What Are People Saying About
I Never Meant to be Funny?

"Every now and then I read something that makes me remember…and contemplate…and laugh, really laugh. **I Never Meant to be Funny** *is such a book. Every daughter and mother and grandmother and reader will relate to the unique, loving, humorous, and clearly human relationships set forth in these stories. So, read them. And allow yourself to remember, contemplate, and laugh, really laugh."*

—Janine Avila

"I read **I Never Meant to be Funny** *and instantly began to relate to its down-to-earth style and presentation of the funny moments in one's life. When we take time to reflect on the simple things in life, we sometimes see how relationships, family, etc. are blessings that are truly enhanced by (with) laughter."*

—Laurie Mahler

*"This book is a great read! It does help knowing one of the 'characters' in the book, but I cannot imagine anyone reading this and not laughing out loud! It is one of those books you read that you will not forget because you **will** repeat the stories. They are written with much love and an uncanny way of making you feel like you are sitting with the storyteller (preferably over a bowl of ice cream). The ability for the storyteller to also laugh at herself shows that both mother and daughter possess a great sense of humor (even if only one is aware of it). ENJOY IT. I did!"*

—Kerrie Adams

"Great mother, daughter family stories told in a loving way that are guaranteed to make you laugh and visualize the moment. Not many families can match this number of funny stories told on themselves. After you quit laughing and enjoying their tales, you will find yourself smiling as you start to reflect on your own family's funny moments."

—Alice Todd

I Never Meant to be Funny

I Never Meant to be Funny

◆

True Mother and Daughter Stories

As Told By
Karen R. Shulman

iUniverse, Inc.
New York Lincoln Shanghai

I Never Meant to be Funny
True Mother and Daughter Stories

iUniverse, Inc.

For information address:
iUniverse, Inc.
2021 Pine Lake Road, Suite 100
Lincoln, NE 68512
www.iuniverse.com

ISBN: 0-595-30596-2

Printed in the United States of America

I dedicate this book to my mother, Micki, who continues to be an inspiration, teacher, friend, and the subject of wonderful stories.

Contents

Foreword. xv

I Never Meant to be Funny: True Mother and Daughter Stories

CHAPTER 1   Cases of Mistaken Identity 3

CHAPTER 2   My Mother and the Five (Or More?) Senses 6

  • *Hearing Challenges* *6*

  • *Speaking Challenges*. *8*

  • *Visual Challenges*. *9*

  • *Tactile Challenges* *11*

  • *Taste Challenges (Sort Of)* *12*

CHAPTER 3   On a More Serious Note (Well, Kind Of) 13

CHAPTER 4   Embarrassing Moments. 16

CHAPTER 5   Travel 20

CHAPTER 6   Matters of Mothering 29

CHAPTER 7   The Kindergarten Teacher. .42

CHAPTER 8   Could It Be Hereditary?. 45

Conclusion 75

Do You Have A Funny 'Mother Story' Of Your Own To Share? 79

Acknowledgments

It took a fair amount of prompting by others for me to sit down and finally write this book and pursue its publication.

For all the friends and clients who laughed with me as I've told all my 'mother stories' over the years, thank you for your encouragement, support, and sense of humor. In order to bring these stories to the public, I was ultimately going to have to write a book or create a stand-up-comedy routine. I chose to go the book route, thinking it would be a quicker option; I'm not exactly sure that this was the case.

Mindy, and Geoff, our plan to write together never came to be (at least as of this writing). However, you were huge reasons why this book was written.

Without a deadline looming over me, I know this book would not have been written so soon. So, thank you Aunt Joanie and Uncle Paul for planning and throwing my parents the party that inspired me to put all these stories on paper.

Thank you to my "test-market": my friends, family, and clients, who have waited for *I Never Meant to be Funny* so that they could finally read my creation. Your feedback was invaluable, and I love that you have had fun with your read.

If Kris, my friend and marketing specialist, had not been so excited about *I Never Meant to be Funny* as a project, I probably would not have gone the formal publishing route.

If my mother would not have loved the manuscript of this book so much, I might not have been so willing to share it with everyone. Thank you, Ma, for encouraging me to get it published.

Honey Anne, you're always our family's leading-lady. Thank you for rarely *trying* to be funny.

Marla, thank you for your artistic eye and words of encouragement.

My brother is the true writer in the family. His editing and creativity were invaluable in the process of sending the final product to print. Eric, thank you for helping me to be a better writer.

Connie, thank you for proofreading the manuscript. You are speedy!

Beckie and Paddy, you have sacrificed time for me and listened to me talk incessantly about my book. Thank you for your support and patience.

And last, but certainly not least, thank you, Veronica, for opening me up to a much more enlightened path in life. You are my angel.

I love all of you who have played roles, however large or small, in the creation of this book. Thank you so much for being in my life and for making my days here on earth joyful.

Foreword

Mothers. They teach us many wonderful things, like how to walk, talk, eat, drink and clean up. A bit later, they teach us about writing, reading, doing arithmetic, maybe even speaking foreign languages, and driving cars. Mothers try to show us things like how to be good citizens, responsible, respectful, family-oriented and caring. Ultimately, we learn from watching them.

My mother taught me all of these things. Well, not arithmetic. Oh, and certainly not foreign languages. But she did a fine job on all the others.

One of the most valuable lessons my mother taught me was how to laugh. As I was growing up, we laughed at funny stories and jokes. As I got older, we laughed at each other. No wait—that's not true. I laughed at *her*. I didn't like people laughing at *me*. And, I didn't laugh at her alone. She laughed right along with me.

It wasn't until later in my life that my mother provided me with the most wonderful lesson of all. My mother taught me how to laugh at myself. When she did something a bit silly, she'd make it into a story over which we could all share a laugh. And she probably laughed the loudest of us all.

Finally, the stories of my mother's laughableness have become this book. After all, our family has told these stories over and over again to hundreds of people, until they have become legends. Other families and friends have been privy to hearing some of the stories, but even they have probably not heard all of them.

For years, I have threatened my mom, telling her that some day I was going to write a book about all the 'mother stories' (referred to by some as "Micki-isms") I could remember.

My step-dad, Sam, has referred to my mom as the funniest woman alive. He feels that way because she is a riot, without ever really intending to be. I don't know if she's the funniest woman alive. But I guarantee you, many of these stories will make you laugh. Not just a chuckle, but full belly laughs from deep inside. You go right ahead and give it a full belly laugh, too. After all, my mom taught me it was OK to laugh at others as long as they were laughing at themselves.

To sum up my mother's great attitude, I include this: Once, not too long ago I told her, "Ma, you're a great sport. You do some of the craziest things and you just laugh at yourself."

As she laughed, her response was, "What choice do I have?"

I love my mother very dearly. She is a wonderful teacher, role model, and friend. Truly a good person, she is a kind soul, full of love and energy. Everyone who knows her just loves her, but they don't necessarily know the side of her that I want to share with you in this book. If Micki is already dear to you, then this book will enhance the feelings you have for her. If you don't know her personally, you'll feel like you do after you read this. This book will let you into a part of my mother's life and will hopefully teach you, as it has taught me, the valuable lesson of learning to laugh at our own quirks, flaws, faults, zaniness, and silliness.

These stories are truthfully told (I don't think I could make them up, even if I wanted to) to the best of my recollection. There is minimal, if any, embellishment. I have told them the way I remember them happening. Admittedly, some names have been changed to protect the innocent or partners in silliness. And, in case you think I failed in the life lesson of respectfulness, there is a chapter on heredity where I share with you that I am my mother's daughter (and my grandmother's granddaughter).

So why did I write *I Never Meant to be Funny*? Was it to fulfill a threat I made years ago? Frankly, this may have been sufficient motivation. Over the last few years, I have evolved into a much more open person. I have learned that stories about mothers, grandmothers—even about myself—are funny to me and to others, and I truly feel that there is simply not enough laughter in the world today.

If this book adds a little laughter to your life, then it has served its purpose. If this book encourages you to share stories and laughter with others, then it has doubled its purpose. If *I Never Meant to be Funny* inspires you to record stories of your own then it has truly been worth all the effort. If *I Never Meant to be Funny* initiates a stronger connection between you and others, then it has facilitated enjoyment of one of life's greatest gifts. We are all human beings, with all our various qualities—what I like to call 'The Good, The Bad, and The Funny'—why not share the fun stuff?

When you've finished *I Never Meant to be Funny*, you'll find a fun challenge awaiting you. Why not write down your stories and share them? If you'd like to share your stories with my readers, follow the guide at the back of this book that will help you send them to me, and I may include them in future editions of *I Never Meant to be Funny*.

Enjoy your read. It was fun to witness these stories, and still more fun writing it all down for you.

I Never Meant
to be Funny:
True Mother and
Daughter Stories

o o o o o o o o o o o o o o o o o o o o o o o o o o o o o o o o o o

Blessed are those who can laugh at themselves, for they shall never cease to be amused.

—Author Unknown

1

Cases of Mistaken Identity

When I was about twelve, our family took a nice summer vacation to California. We did it right. We went from San Francisco to Los Angeles taking the scenic tour—Highway One—and stopped in lots of great places. The last part of our trip was in Los Angeles. Tired from all that driving, we decided to hang out at the hotel's rooftop pool.

My mother, who is always sure we will see somebody we know everywhere we go, scanned the rooftop for a familiar face. And, wonder of wonders, she saw an old friend from high school, a guy by the name of Darby Cato. She and Darby started chatting and reminiscing, while I just relaxed and caught some rays.

After a few minutes, I heard her say to Darby, "Let me introduce you to my daughter. Darby, this is my daughter Karen; Karen, this is my friend Darby Cato from school."

I said the obligatory "hi" and hoped to get back to my sun-bathing, but apparently that was out of the question.

My mother's voice once again interrupted my sun-bath. "Karen, I'm sure you've met Darby before, haven't you? You and I have gone into his office supply store, and I'm sure I introduced the two of you."

"No, Ma, that wasn't me. I know where Cato's Office Supply is located, but I've never been there before. Maybe it was [my brother] Rick that went with you, but it wasn't me," I offered.

"Well *sure* it was you, honey. I remember talking to you when we were going into the store," she replied.

I repeated my case. "Ma, it wasn't me. I swear I've never been in Mr. Cato's store before."

She thought about it for a few seconds and admitted, "You're right. It wasn't you that went with me that day. It was Fren-Lee, our dog."

Considering my resemblance to a Lhasa-Apso, no wonder she was confused!

3

◆   ◆   ◆

I once called my mother on a weeknight evening to say hello. When she answered the phone, I began with my usual, "Hi, Ma. How ya' doin'?"

To my astonishment, she responded, "I think you have the wrong number. What number are you trying to call?"

Thinking that she wanted to horse around a bit, I appeased her playful sense of humor by rattling off her phone number in a sing-song fashion.

She then said in a somewhat perplexed tone, "Well, I *do* believe you have the right number, but I *don't* believe I'm your mother!"

In my mind, I still thought there was a slim chance that she was pulling my leg. So, I asked, "Is this Micki?"

She answered, "Why yes, it is."

I then inquired, "And, do you have a daughter named Karen Shulman?"

She responded, "Why yes, I do."

At this point, I figured the joke was on her, not me. She wasn't pulling my leg; she was clueless as to who I was. Despite the fact that I have a very distinct voice, and even people who have only spoken to me once on the phone can readily identify me the second time they hear my voice, my own mother did not recognize me on the phone this particular night. So, I went in for the finish. I exclaimed, "Ma, this would be me...your daughter...Karen Shulman. It's me, Ma."

As she laughed and screamed at her blunder, she tried to do some explaining. She offered, "Oh, it didn't sound like you. We have company over for dinner, and it's very loud in here. I wasn't expecting a call from you tonight. I was going to call you later." Then, in the midst of the laughter from my stepfather, Sam, and their company (who were able to decipher at their end what happened during the conversation), I heard my stepfather yelling, "You think that's bad. Try waking up with her in the morning. She turns over, looks at me and says 'who the hell are you?'"

The story doesn't end there. A few weeks later I flew to Florida to visit my folks. With me I took a sign that said, "I'm looking for Micki. I am your daughter." I carried it with me into the baggage claim area, our pre-arranged meeting location. I believe my mother recognized me when she saw me, but she scrunched up her face and strained her eyes to read my sign. As she approached, I could see her reading and mouthing the words of the sign. She then smacked me in the arm and told me, "You think you're funny, don't you?"

I said that indeed I did. The sign was my only way of insuring that she knew I was the person she was supposed to take home with her for a few days.

◆   ◆   ◆

The story did end there, temporarily. Five years later, my mother called me to tell me about a sequel, of sorts:

"Hi, Karen. How are you doing?" my mom asked me.

"Good, Ma. How about you?" I said in response.

"I'm good, too. I just tried to call you," my mother stated.

The phone hadn't rung at my house. How could she have just tried to call me? "Ma, the phone never rang here. What happened?" I asked.

"It appears I dialed a wrong number. You know I have a cell phone where I've programmed your number in the speed dial, right?" she explained.

I answered, "Right, Ma."

"Well, for some reason I didn't use the speed dial," she said, and then she paused. "And, I have a cell phone that would allow me to say 'call Karen', but I didn't use that, either. I just dialed. I don't know why, but I just dialed your number."

"So what happened?" I inquired.

"Well," my mother continued, "a woman answered the phone, and she sounded a bit like you. I said, 'Hi, Karen. How are you?' The woman said, 'Who are you trying to call?' and I thought you were teasing me, you know, paying me back for when I didn't know it was you on the phone."

By this time, we were both giggling, because she and I both knew I wasn't playing a joke on her. "Yeah? Keep going, Ma," I urged.

"So, I kept playing along with the woman, thinking it was you. 'I'm trying to call my daughter. Are you my daughter?' That's what I asked her," continued my mother. "Then the woman says to me, 'Not that I know of.' Now, I still thought it was you, Karen, pulling one over on me. So, I said to her, 'Are you writing a book about me?'"

"And then what happened, Ma?" I asked, because I knew we had to be near the end of the latest 'mother story'.

My mother exclaimed, "The woman hung up on me!"

We were both laughing so hard, we were crying. "Ma," I said. "I'm still putting the finishing touches on the book before I send it to the publisher. I'm glad I haven't turned it in yet, because this needs to be added. Thanks for sharing!"

2

My Mother and the Five (Or More?) Senses

HEARING CHALLENGES

My mother has a history of being what I like to call 'audibly challenged'. Many of her funniest moments occur when she hears things incorrectly. You may think this is from a medical problem or age-related hearing loss. No, don't think that at all. This started at an early age…relatives say it began in her childhood, and is uniquely Micki.

I asked my mom about getting a hearing test once. She said she'd already had one. Her hearing was perfect, according to the test. So I asked her, "How could that be?"

She answered, "Well, I can hear sounds and pitches of tones. I just can't make out words. Maybe they need to develop a different test for what I have."

I remember, as a kid, my friends Steve and Jeff coming over to play. They rang the bell and my brother answered the door. He told Steve and Jeff he'd go get me and tell me to join them outside. While he was trying to find me, our mother yelled from upstairs, "Rick, who's at the door?"

My brother shouted back from the bottom of the stairs, "Steve and Jeff are at the door."

My mother shouted, "A trumpet is at the door?" (Can you even picture a trumpet walking up to your door and ringing the bell? Nope? Me either.)

The distance from our front door to the top of the stairs was not that great. There were no jackhammers blasting inside or near the house. There wasn't even a radio playing or TV blaring anywhere. How she got "trumpet" from "Steve and Jeff" remains a mystery to this day.

◆   ◆   ◆

A more recent example of hearing challenges is contained in the following little ditty. A few summers back, I was entertaining relatives and friends for a girls' sleepover. We decided to go out for dinner and had a great time at a Chinese restaurant. On the way home, my cousin admired the beautiful, older homes near my neighborhood. One of the homes had been converted into a museum, and as my cousin read the sign over the entranceway, she had a question. The museum was called the Huggins Maritime Museum, and unfamiliar with the term "maritime" my cousin asked, "What's a merry-time museum?"

My mother jumped in with the bold enthusiasm of the amateur historian and exclaimed breathlessly, "You have a Mary Todd Museum? Mary Todd was born in Toledo, Ohio? I didn't know that Mary Todd was from Toledo and that you had a museum to honor her. Have you ever *been* there?"

The uproarious laughter in the car was almost deafening. My mother didn't understand. We were laughing so hard that she started laughing too. She finally asked, "What's so funny? Did I say something funny? Have I done another 'mother story'?"

It took every bit of self-control to continue driving the car, trying to see through the tears in my eyes, and trying to remain upright, as opposed to collapsing, doubled over with laughter. Luckily, we arrived home safely.

◆   ◆   ◆

Here is a more recent incident. Sam and my mother were at home relaxing one evening. The phone rang, and, contrary to typical protocol, my stepfather answered the phone. He spoke to the caller, turned to my mother and said, "It's Felice."

My mom anxiously responded, "It's the police! What do they want with us?"

Sam, through his laughter, said, "I said it was your friend, Felice, not the police."

"Oh, that's very different," she replied. "Let me talk to her."

◆   ◆   ◆

SPEAKING CHALLENGES

As you can tell from the other stories, my mother has a tendency to get excited and speak before she thinks. Sometimes it's not just her hearing that's a problem.

One of these speaking challenges stories occurred long before my brother and I were even thought of; it happened when my mother and father were dating. One night, back in the late 1950s, my dad thought it would be great fun to take his fiancée to a Detroit Red Wing hockey game at the old Olympia Arena. As was typical back then, my father was running late. He and my mother arrived in Detroit just a few minutes before the game began. They parked the car and started walking briskly toward the arena. My mother, who always hated to be late, told my father she thought they should start running. At a crosswalk, waiting for the light to change and surrounded by many people, he asked her why they were running. She replied, "We don't want to be late for the *puck-off*."

◆   ◆   ◆

Sometimes my mom will mix up words, and these become classic 'mother stories.' I remember this story from when I was about seven years old:

My grandparents were only in their forties when my brother and I were born—too young, they thought, to be called grandma and grandpa. So, my parents decided that my brother and I would call our grandparents "Honey" followed by their first names. We were lucky; we had four grandparents still living—Honey Anne, Honey Joe, Honey Doris, and Honey Ted.

My brother, for reasons unknown, decided he liked the name "Honey Booby" better than "Honey Anne," and the name stuck. We called my grandmother (Anne) Honey Booby for a number of years after that.

One day as we were taking a ride in the family car, we passed a brown brick building. My mother, playing tour guide, suddenly and enthusiastically announced, "Look, there on the right! There's Honey Beauty's Booby Parlor!"

◆   ◆   ◆

Another example of speaking challenges, which confused my brother and me for years (and may explain why we had tooth and skin problems), started one morning when we were getting ready for school. We were downstairs eating breakfast, and somebody declared it was time to finish getting ready so that we could catch the bus. My brother and I started to head upstairs to finish our morning grooming rituals. On our way upstairs, my mother shouted, "Now kids, before you go, don't forget to brush your faces and comb your teeth."

◆   ◆   ◆

VISUAL CHALLENGES

One night, many years ago, when I was still in college, my mom was meeting a group of her high school girlfriends for dinner. She had mentioned to me that on my way home, I might want to stop and see everybody. I told her that if the timing worked out right, I'd probably do just that.

On my way home that night, I stopped at the restaurant shortly before the group's gathering ended. It was enjoyable to see my mom's long-term friends and meet some that I had never been introduced to before. On the way out, my mom said she'd like to use the rest room. The other ladies said their goodbyes and off they went; I said I would wait for my mom and walk out with her.

When we left the restaurant, it was getting late and very dark. While the parking lot was lit, it wasn't illuminated all that well. I kissed my mom good-bye and started to walk to my car. Suddenly, she whispered loudly to me, "Karen. Stop. What is that man doing over there?"

"What man, Ma? I don't see any man," I whispered back to her.

"That man over there," she explained as she pointed beyond a row of cars to our right.

I really *didn't* see anyone, but I figured I had better not ignore my mother's warning. So, I moved next to her side, to protect her and hear her better. "Mom, I don't see any man. You know me and my less-than-perfect eyesight. Tell me again where you see him," I urged.

She said in a quiet and somewhat frightened tone, "Over there, honey. By the silver car. I think he's crouching."

"Ma," I replied, "I still don't see any man by any car, and certainly not in a crouching position. Let me see if I can get a closer look." I wasn't convinced I wanted to get a closer look, mind you, but I figured we'd be there all night if one of us didn't make a move. And, judging from my mother's level of fear, she wasn't going to be moving forward any time soon.

"Be careful," she warned. "Who knows what he's doing and why he's here. For all we know he could be armed and dangerous."

'Great' I thought to myself. Whatever courage I had mustered up to move a step or two forward was now being challenged by the thought that the man might: 1) actually be there, 2) truly be armed and dangerous, and 3) might be interested in harming me or my mother. Still, I was tired and I really wanted to go home. It was cold outside and the thought of getting into a warm bed and falling fast asleep became more appealing than fearing for my life. So, I ventured a few bold steps forward.

"Can you see him yet? Do you know what he's doing?" my mother whispered with strained fear in her voice.

"I still can't see anyone. I'm going to have to take a few steps closer, Ma," I answered.

"OK, be careful," she ordered.

I'm pretty sure that this was followed by the 'he may be armed and dangerous' comment again, but by this point, I'd decided to tune her out. I was already scared, and that rhetoric of fear wasn't going to help me. I took a deep breath and made a few giant leaps forward to get a better view of our potential perpetrator. I finally saw what she must have thought was a crouching man. Standing up, no longer hiding, I turned around to address my mother. "Ma," I said. "I think it's going to be OK. The crouching man next to the silver car is an evergreen tree. I think we're going to be just fine."

◆   ◆   ◆

To celebrate my fortieth birthday, my mom suggested that she and I do a mother-daughter trip to a place of my choosing. I suggested we go somewhere neither of us had been before—Maine. She agreed, and so, in the summer of 2000 we flew to Maine, rented a car and drove from Portland to Bar Harbor and worked our way back down the coast stopping and staying over at various cities of interest.

Toward the end of our trip, on our way to South Thomaston, we decided to try to find Owl's Head State Park and Lighthouse. We'd spent the whole week getting lost, having a very difficult time reading maps of Maine and finding important road signs, and today was turning out to be no exception. We must have put an extra thousand miles on that rent-a-car just from all the turning around and backtracking we did. Ah, but that's a different 'mother story.'

After many attempts, and hours of circling and backtracking, we finally found our way into the park. We parked the car and started following the path leading us into the trees. We walked for a while, taking in all the surrounding beauty. After about fifteen minutes, we came to a fork in the path. There we encountered a sign that we hoped would help us decide which route to take. My mother, playing tour-guide yet once more, looked at the sign and said to me, "Well, if we go to the left, we can go swimming. And if we go to the right, we can get gasoline."

Now, I admit it—I have weak eyes. I've been wearing glasses since the age of three, and, even with corrective lenses, I still have problems seeing. However, I had no idea where my mother was getting "gasoline" from that sign. So I said, "Ma, I see the swimming part of that sign—the figure of someone swimming—that's the fork to the left, but from where are you getting gasoline?"

She told me, "Look at the right side of that sign. It has a picture of a gasoline pump."

Well, maybe the image on the right side of the sign looked like a gasoline pump to her, but I didn't think so. Besides, what would a gasoline pump be doing in the middle of a state park? I was sure it wasn't gasoline, but I wasn't sure I could trust my eyes. "Ma," I said. "Could we take a few steps closer to that sign? I don't think it's gasoline as much as some other option."

So, we proceeded to take a few steps and get closer to the sign. "Ma, I think I know what the sign is saying. It's not gasoline to the right; I think if you go to the right, you can see a lighthouse."

We're still laughing over that one.

◆   ◆   ◆

TACTILE CHALLENGES

It's amazing how two people can go through the same thing and have totally different perceptions of the experience. Even though my mom and I are similar in many ways, we found a major difference between us a few years back.

My mom started pre-menopause very early, at around the age of thirty-four. I was no different; I started at about the same age. Over the years, I asked my mother questions about her pre-menopausal experience so that I would know if what I was going through was normal or not. Through hot flashes, bitchiness, and periods that went on for weeks and weeks (these only intensified the bitchiness), she was there to answer my questions and offer a loving, listening ear.

A few years ago, I had to have an endometrial biopsy. I remember telling her it was a pretty unpleasant thing. For some reason, a few months after mine, my mom had to have one, too.

After her biopsy, she sent me an email. She wrote, "I remember you telling me about your endometrial biopsy and that it wasn't too much fun. I just had one also. It was so pinchy, it made me want to scream."

I responded to her email with, "You know, we aren't all that much alike. It was so pinchy it made you want to scream? How about my experience? It hurt like hell and I wanted to kick the doctor in the head!"

◆   ◆   ◆

TASTE CHALLENGES (SORT OF)

OK, this story is a short one that could actually be classified as a speaking challenge, but my editor told me I needed to put something under the heading of taste.

This happened so long ago, that I really don't remember what events led up to my mom's ever-important declaration. So, I'll make something up. We were probably discussing what to have for dinner. My brother and I probably wanted some kind of fast food. My dad probably wanted Chinese food. My mom probably didn't really care. Then we all probably started throwing in ideas of all different types of food. Somebody suggested pizza. My mother then declared, "I don't know if I want pizza. After all, I get pizzas from eating pimples."

Ugh, I know, but it's proof that all of this started way back when.

3

On a More Serious Note (Well, Kind Of)

In November of 1995, my mother was diagnosed with breast cancer. While this might be a paralyzing diagnosis for most people, my mother demonstrated incredible courage and, of course, humor throughout her cancer challenges. When she called to tell me that she had found a cancerous lump and that she was going to have a mastectomy, we cried together and we laughed together.

I remember her asking me if I needed any new bras. And I replied, "Well, yeah, why?"

She said that she had just purchased several new bras and bathing suits, and she didn't want them to go to waste. She wanted to know if I could use them.

Now, I'm not very well endowed, if you know what I mean. Although she's no Dolly Parton, I pale in comparison to my mother, so, I asked her (somewhat tentatively because I wasn't sure how it was going to land), "Did you have the bras and suits sized for you pre-or post-mastectomy?"

She replied, not yet knowing exactly where I was going with my question, "Pre-. Why would you ask that?"

I answered, and held my breath for a second after I finished, "Well, the only way those bras and suits are going to fit me is if you sized them for yourself post-mastectomy, Ma!"

We howled with laughter, and we cried over that one.

◆　　　◆　　　◆

My mother had her mastectomy in January of 1996. I went to Florida to help with her recuperation after surgery. When she came home from the hospital, she looked tired—understandably so. She was lying in bed and asked me if I wanted to see her scar. When I told her that I would, she pulled up her pajama top, and I

13

saw two red tubes and two round things attached at each tube's end. These funny-looking, plastic contraptions were attached to her side. I asked, "What are those?"

My mother explained their function, first. "They're drainage tubes, and the round containers at the end of the tubes are collecting vessels for the excess fluid."

Not quite through with her explanation at that point, she summed it up, as only my mother could do, by saying, "Can you believe it? I go to the hospital and what happens? I trade a boob for two balls!"

Needless to say, I knew she'd recover just fine from her surgery.

◆   ◆   ◆

I'm not sure what I expected during my mother's recuperation from her mastectomy surgery, but I thought, in some ways, she'd be a changed woman. In fact, I noticed, interestingly enough, that she was acting pretty normal—for her. She welcomed, joked, and talked with her many visitors, had a robust appetite, and maintained a positive outlook on life. If there was any change at all, it was merely that she was more tired than usual.

A few days after her surgery, she came out of her bedroom shaking her head in disbelief. I asked her what was wrong. She said, "You see the way I've been eating these last few days; I'm eating everything is sight, but I don't get it. I just weighed myself, and I've lost weight."

"How much weight did you loose, Ma?" I asked.

"Oh, about four pounds" she said.

I countered with, "Oh really, and that's a surprise?"

She said, "Well, yes, it is. With all the cookies and candies that people have sent in as well as the neighbors preparing us full meals, of which I'm eating everything, how could I be losing weight?"

"Ma", I said. "Think about it. Did you just have a body part removed?"

"Well, yes, I did" she responded.

"OK, well how much do you think a boob weighs, Ma?" I asked.

"Hmm…maybe about four pounds?" she offered sheepishly.

◆   ◆   ◆

A few years after my mother's surgery, there was a "WARNING" email going around that went something like this:

> Warning! Warning! If a man comes to your door and asks to see your boobs, don't show him your boobs. The only reason he's there is to see your boobs. I repeat, don't show him your boobs.
>
> I wish somebody had told me that yesterday before he came to my door.

I sent this email to my mother and to several of my friends. My mother sent an email back to me that said, "Too late. He was already here. The surprise was on him, though. I don't think he'll be back. When I lifted my shirt, I only had one."

4

Embarrassing Moments

My mother is such a good sport about all her funny-isms, that she rarely becomes embarrassed. Mostly, she just laughs along with the crowd (whoever is there to witness the goings on) or even laughs at herself if she's alone. Yet there have been a few occasions when she has actually experienced a sense of embarrassment.

When I was growing up, we had wonderful friends, Alvin and Judy, who had us over to their house to swim in their pool just about every summer weekend. Alvin and Judy always invited such a fun crowd, which included their neighbors, relatives, and friends. You never knew who would be there. We were forever meeting new people and seeing others who became weekend fixtures at Alvin and Judy's household, too. It was a blast spending the entire weekend in your bathing suit just having fun. We all have great memories of our times together at the "Alvin and Judy Swim Club."

My set-up of the "Alvin and Judy Swim Club" might lead you to believe that what follows is totally unrelated, but just bear with me.

My grandfather's business once had a huge holiday party to which our family was invited. It was a big bash where employees, customers, suppliers, and family dressed up, ate, drank, danced, and had a fabulous time. I have to say that I didn't witness first-hand what I'm going to tell you next. Actually, nobody in our family witnessed this first-hand, other than my mother, who told it to us laughing.

As my mom stood in line to get a plate of food, the gentleman next to her started a conversation. As she told it later, he was very friendly and started talking to her like he knew her. She tried to place him, but just couldn't. As they continued talking, she hoped her brain would be able to identify him. Unfortunately, her memory synapses were firing at less than 100 percent that evening, so, being an honest person, she finally admitted to the man, "I have to confess. You look very familiar, and I probably know you. But, I just can't place you. Who are you?"

The man told her his name and my mother still couldn't place him. She said, "I'm really sorry. I know I *know* you, but I just don't know *how* I know you."

He then explained to her, "Well, Micki, we've met a dozen or more times swimming at Alvin and Judy's. I'm their next door neighbor."

My mother, who was so relieved to finally understand how she knew this man, loudly exclaimed, "I knew I knew you. I just didn't recognize you with your clothes on!"

◆   ◆   ◆

This next story recalls an embarrassing moment for my mother, as she dined one night with Sam and four other couples. To top it off, I played a practical joke on her afterward that may have helped that embarrassment sink in just a bit more.

I was home from college for the weekend and was having friends over to play cards. My folks were going out to dinner and then to one of the couples' homes for dessert. My mom told me that in between dinner and dessert they would probably stop back at the house, just to say hi to my friends, and me.

My friends and I were playing a fierce game of Buck'Em, when my parents returned to say their hellos. While they were home, my mom told me that she had done another 'mother story' at dinner. My eyes lit up. I loved it when she told stories of herself, and especially if there was an audience with whom to laugh. She proceeded to tell us what happened at dinner. She said that everyone had ordered their meals, and that they were talking about one thing or another and munching on bread. The waiter soon delivered the first course, salad. Everyone dug in and continued on with their conversation. Soon afterward, the main courses were served, and my mother got a perplexed look on her face. She asked the waiter why she had not been given her salad. He explained that he had already brought salads to everyone.

"You didn't bring me *my* salad," she exclaimed.

"Why, yes, ma'm, I did. I brought your salad and cleared the plate away after you had finished, just like I did for the rest of your table," he answered politely.

My mom started to protest some more, but there were about nine eyewitnesses at her table who made her stop. They all confirmed what the waiter had said, adding that they had all watched her get and eat her salad. After that, she had no choice but to back down. She apologized to the waiter for her mistake.

My friends and I laughed with her as she concluded her story. Soon, she and Sam were off to the Garber's for dessert, and then I had a brainstorm. I quickly got out the phone book and found the Garber's number. I dialed and talked to Mr. Garber, who I hadn't seen since I was little. I explained who I was, and he said that my folks were not there yet. I told him that they were on their way. We chit-chatted for a few minutes and then I got down to business.

"Mr. Garber," I said, "Do you have any salad in your refrigerator?"

I heard him yell to his wife to inquire. He came back to the phone and said, "Yes, we have some lettuce and some other salad stuff. Why?"

I told him I needed to play a practical joke on my mother by having him serve her a salad instead of dessert. He became very enthused about the joke and promised to carry out the mission.

When my folks got home, I heard how unappreciative my mom was about my practical joke, but she was smiling the whole time she was attempting to ball me out.

◆   ◆   ◆

Embarrassing and funny things happen to my mother even when she's not really in the picture, so to speak. This story will illustrate the point:

My mom was going to do her good deed for the day. One of her friends was moving soon, and my mom thought she'd go to the grocery store early in the morning to pick up some good egg or banana boxes for her. She's always liked the strong boxes with handles. When my mom arrived at the grocery store very early in the morning, the parking lot was quite empty. She knew she could just run into the store quickly and get some boxes, and she did. She loaded the boxes in a shopping cart and wheeled them out to the parking lot.

Concentrating hard, my mom tried to make sure the cart did not hit any walls, people, or any other animate or inanimate objects. As she wheeled the cart from the walkway in front of the store to the parking lot, she looked both ways to check for traffic.

She was practicing what she had preached all those years to all of her kids (my brother, me, and generations of kindergarten students). She then decided to look forward, toward her car. When she did, she saw a car heading straight for her Honda. She yelled, "Stop! Stop! Please, stop! You're going to hit my car!"

But the car kept moving, with dead-on aim for my mother's Honda. There wasn't another automobile in the parking lot, mind you, just my mother's. With the driver obviously ignoring her, and my mother's irritation and anxiety growing, she started to run toward the moving vehicle, yelling louder, "Stop! Stop! You're going to hit my car!"

By this time, mom was racing at blazing speed and had actually caught up with the rolling car. She yelled, "Stop, you idiot! Stop! Hit the brake before you hit my car!" As she looked into the driver's side window, she noticed that there was an empty space. There wasn't a soul driving that car (which explained why the driver ignored her desperate pleas). At this point, she also noticed that there was nothing she could do except watch the rolling car smack into hers! My mother had just experienced a collision with her car and another vehicle, and absolutely no drivers were involved! How many people have *that* claim to fame?

In case you were wondering, it turned out that the driver of the other car had just run inside to a beauty shop. The woman figured it would only take a few seconds, so she left her car running and, she thought, in PARK. Obviously, that was not the case. There have been problems with some car models every once in a while disengaging from PARK. My mom's car was hit by one. Damage was approximately $500. This story? Priceless!

I wish I could tell you that it was my mom's friend, the one for whom she was doing the good deed, who owned the runaway car, because that would have made the story even funnier. But, it wasn't, so I can't.

5

Travel

Not everyone is a barrel of laughs to be with when they travel. My mother, on the other hand, is a barrel-and-a half. Some would call her paranoid and fearful while traveling, but I prefer to interpret the following as evidence that my mom is a great source of vacation entertainment.

In the summer of 1992, thirteen members of our family took a trip to Israel together. My grandmother (my mom's mom), my mom and Sam, my two uncles and their wives (my mom's brothers and sisters-in-law), four of my first cousins, one of their spouses (my mom's nieces and nephews), and I all made the trip. Essentially, we rented a tour bus and hired a guide for the majority of our travels across the country. We really had fun and got to know each other better by spending a lot of time together.

Admittedly, it was a little scary being in a foreign country. We were in Israel, a country that has violent struggles with its neighbors. We saw armed soldiers everywhere we went, and it was a little unsettling at first. After a while, however, we started to get used to the culture, and realized that we were probably safer in Israel than in America (at least, that was the case back in 1992).

But not everyone on our trip felt that way. My mother was on guard most of the time during the trip. She was convinced we were going to be attacked by terrorists at any moment. And, since none of the rest of us felt that way, she took it upon herself to be vigilant for our group. How lucky we were that she took on that role, because it made for some great stories.

The first memorable story was when we toured Massada, a mountain near the Dead Sea that was the site of an intense battle (between a handful of Jewish rebels and a host of Roman soldiers) years and years and years ago. At the time of our visit, to get up to the top of Massada, one could either walk or take a cable car; the only way down was by cable car. Our family was split on a method of going up the mountain. Five of us younglings and my Uncle Paul all walked; the others rode the cable car.

When we all finally arrived at the top, our tour guide, Chayim, called us over to a covered area with benches. We gathered to listen to him tell the history of Massada. About five minutes into his talk, I became distracted. My mother was acting very weird, even for her. I kept watching her as she observed a stranger; a dark-complected woman in a flowered dress, who was also sitting in the covered area. The woman didn't look at all suspicious, and seemed to be minding her own business.

Soon my mother's watchful gaze became a glare. She whispered to me in an angry tone, "What is that woman *doing*?"

"I think she's trying to listen to Chayim's lecture, just like the rest of us," I replied.

"Oh, no!" she insisted, "Look at her. She keeps going into her purse, then closing her eyes and praying. I don't like the looks of her."

"Mom, I think you're over-reacting. She seems OK to me," I offered.

Since I would not join in her conspiracy theory, my mother continued to glare at the woman and mutter to herself under her breath. Soon, Chayim's lecture was over and we all stood up to tour the twenty acres of ruins that lay before us. The woman in the flowered dress stood up, too. She asked if anyone spoke Spanish. With hand gestures and some broken English, she explained that she had a tape recorder that was not working. My cousin Mindy went over to the woman and tried to help her. Out of nowhere rushed my mother, the Terrorist Avenger. "We have to go now, Mindy!" my mother said rather forcefully. Mindy had no idea what to make of my mother's reaction.

I knew what my mother was up to; I'd seen the panic and anger rising in her for the past several minutes, but everyone else was clueless. The men in our group all decided to try to help the woman by looking at, and attempting to fix, her broken tape recorder.

This was the closest I had ever seen my mother to stroking out. "Don't help her! Don't help her! That may not really be a tape recorder. There could be a bomb in that machine!" Nobody saw the danger that the Terrorist Avenger saw. Everybody (including the Israeli guide) was ignoring the Terrorist Avenger's pleas to get away from the woman in the flowered dress.

Luckily, for my mother (the EXASPERATED Terrorist Avenger at this point), nobody was able to help the woman fix her tape recorder. We did not blow up, my mother calmed down, and we were able to finish our tour of Massada safely. We had been warned, though. The Terrorist Avenger had only just begun her crusade.

◆   ◆   ◆

These next two stories occurred on the same day, a non-touring day when many of us ventured out in small groups to check out the shopping in Jerusalem. I spent a few hours with my cousins Marla and Robbie shopping on Ben Yehudah Street, and then lunching at the Burger Barn Restaurant, Israel's attempt at fast food (not a very good attempt, either). We then went back to the hotel to swim, sun-bathe, read, and play Scrabble. That evening, I went to dinner with my folks, to a restaurant called The Classic Diner. On the way in, I noticed a lot of people standing at a bus stop. It was a very hot evening, and I was glad to be going inside, out of the intense sunshine.

Once seated at our table, my mother started to interrogate my stepfather and me about the terrorist outside the restaurant. "Which terrorist would that be, Ma?" I asked.

"The man leaning against the pole outside across the street," she replied. "Didn't you see him?"

"Describe him, Ma, would you? There were lots of people outside across the street," I said.

"Sam, you should know who I'm talking about. It's the same man we've seen all day. Every shop we went into, he was there outside. Every shop we came out of, he was there waiting, and standing," said my mother.

"I don't know who you are talking about, Mick," replied my stepfather.

"He's right outside. He's a skinny, unshaven, sweaty man leaning against a pole near the bus stop," she explained.

"Mick, you've just described ninety percent of the men in this country. Relax! He's not a terrorist, and he's certainly not following us," reasoned Sam.

"Look, I know *that man* is not right. I know he's up to no good. I don't know what he wants with us, but I'm sure he's after us. He made eye contact with me on the way into the restaurant. I think that was a warning signal. He had better not be out there when we finish dinner," she protested. After all, she was the Terrorist Avenger and that meant trouble for him.

"Ma," I offered. "Maybe he made eye contact with you because after all your chance meetings with him today, he thinks you look familiar to him?"

With that, my mom actually laughed and started to relax. She even dropped it. We were able to eat dinner peacefully and without the threat or talk of terrorism. And, fortunately for us, *that man* was not waiting for us when we left the restaurant.

◆   ◆   ◆

After dinner at The Classic Diner, we were to meet with the rest of the family on Ben Yehudah Street. We decided to walk from the restaurant, since the sun had gone down, and the wind provided a nice, strong breeze. The temperature was very pleasant. We took in the sights around us and walked at a nice, relaxed pace. About two blocks from Ben Yehudah Street, my mom stopped abruptly and, like a grade-school safety patrol girl protecting people crossing a street, held out her arms in front of my stepfather and me. "Stop," she exclaimed! "Don't move! What are those people doing up there?"

If you've never been to Ben Yehudah Street, it's a really crowded place. Hundreds of people are on the street or in shops, listening to music, eating at outdoor cafes, and just plain having a great time. So, I wasn't really sure about whom my mother was speaking, but I had a strong suspicion that the Terrorist Avenger part of her personality was kicking in again. "Ma," I asked. "Which people?"

"The people up there to the right," she answered.

"That really narrows it down for me. How about you, Sam?" I asked. (Yes, I was being a smart ass, but I was getting a bit tired of the terrorist warnings.)

"No, I don't know who you're taking about either, Mick," he said.

"Up about three blocks. The people that are dancing, up there on the right, that's who I'm talking about," she said.

Remember, I'm not known for having good eyesight. Conversely, Sam has 20/20 vision. So, I deferred to him, since I didn't know who she meant and I certainly couldn't see anybody dancing.

"Mick, I don't see anyone dancing," he offered.

"OK, let's get a little closer. Take a few steps forward, and that should help you both," she replied.

We took a few steps forward. That didn't help me in the least. I was about to take a few more steps, but my mother, the safety patrol girl, lunged forward and protected us behind her outstretched arms again.

"There, do you see them now? The people dancing up there on the right! They're on the sidewalk, and they're dancing furiously," she further explained.

I was still clueless, and judging from my stepfather's expression, he wasn't seeing her latest terrorists either.

"Ma, I think we're both still missing what you're seeing. Where are you seeing these furiously dancing people?" I asked.

"Up there on the right. They're wearing orange ponchos, and they're dancing crazily," she responded.

All of a sudden, I saw what she saw, and I knew what she was talking about. I had been on that very block earlier in the day with my cousins. I knew, however, that what she was seeing was not a group of people in orange ponchos dancing wildly. "Ma," I retorted, "Those are not people in orange ponchos dancing. Those are the umbrellas on the patio of the Burger Barn Restaurant!"

With that explanation, my mother, the Terrorist Avenger, hung up her cape and retired permanently from that line of work.

◆   ◆   ◆

As part of the Travel chapter, I have to go back to the trip to Maine for my fortieth birthday. My mom and I took this trip about eight years after our trip to Israel. As a precursor to this story, I have to tell you a bit about my roommate and pets. Again, I know this seems absolutely unrelated, but trust me, it's not.

In the late 1990s, I lived with a roommate, Deb, and a dog, Sidney. Sidney was a longhaired Chihuahua, and was pretty much a one-person dog. Deb was an absolute dog lover, and, while she and Sidney got along, he just never really felt like hers to her.

We got a call one day from some friends, who told us that they had found a stray dog on their porch—"nicest dog in the world, sweet, great with other dogs and cats, a real find"—but they didn't want to keep her. They already had two dogs and two cats, and just couldn't take in another pet. They thought Deb might want the dog, since she'd said she'd love to get one of her own. We picked up the dog, which had been named Whiskey, and brought her home. After a bit of a rough start, Sidney and Whiskey got along very well and enjoyed each other's company. Whiskey *was* a nice dog; everything our friends had said was true. But, Deb didn't like the name Whiskey.

A few days after picking up Whiskey, I had my family over for a Memorial Day barbeque. Everyone was excited to get together and to see the new dog. Nobody else thought she looked like a Whiskey, either, but no new name ideas came forward. When my mother went to leave, she said good-bye to Deb, Sidney, and me and went over to Whiskey. She held the dog's face lovingly in her hands and said, "Oy, what a face. What a *shayna punim!*"

Deb, who is not Jewish, turned to me and said, "What did your mom call her?"

I said, "*shayna punim*. It means 'pretty face' in Yiddish."

"Ooohhhh, I like that," said Deb. "I think your mom just named my dog. Shayna. Yep, that'll be her name from now on."

OK, so that's the lead-in. Now, here's the rest of the story, and connection to the Maine trip:

My mom wanted the trip to be very special, and she wanted to plan the whole thing. It was more challenging than she expected, however, since neither of us had been to Maine before, nor had any of her Florida neighbors. My mom wasn't getting too far with travel plans, so I talked with some of my clients. Several had been to Maine and offered suggestions on where to go, what to see, and places to stay. One of my clients had just returned from Maine and had a wonderful travel book about the state. I borrowed it, so that I could help my mom out a bit.

The book was very informative. It had lots of good details that I was able to skim through; I found a page headed "The Top Things to Do and See When in Maine." I bookmarked it; next time I spoke with my mother about the trip, I would be sure to read her that page.

My mom called a few days later, and we started talking about our trip. I told her about the book and said I'd run get it and be right back. I came back to the phone with the book and sat myself down on the floor. Thumbing through the book's pages, I told my mom to hang on. I was locating that page I'd marked, when all of a sudden Shayna playfully approached me and started licking my face. She was having a good time expressing her love for me, but she was getting in the way of my finding the page in the book. So I said, "Shayna, honey. Shayna, honey."

I then heard my mother ask, "Shaynahoney? Shaynahoney, Maine? Where's that? I never heard of it. What's it known for?"

It was another one of those times I thought she was pulling my leg. I honestly thought she understood what was going on at my end of the phone, but obviously that wasn't the case. "Ma," I said. "I was trying to find the page in the book, and somebody here thought I was getting on the ground to play with them. Do you know who that somebody might be?"

"Oh," she replied. "That might be Deb's dog, Shayna. I guess there is no Shaynahoney, Maine, is there?"

"Oh, there might be, Ma, but it's not in the book I have, and it's not on "The Top Things to Do and See When in Maine" page. But, it is another 'mother story,' isn't it?" I replied.

"Yes, I guess it is," she admitted as she laughed with me.

◆   ◆   ◆

As you've probably realized by now, some of my mother's stories become 'mother stories' because of the practical jokes I play. After "Shaynahoney, Maine", I knew I had to play a practical joke on my mother while we traveled together. But, what to pull on her and how to pull it off remained mysterious to me for a while.

I believe it was one of my friends who suggested that I make Shaynahoney, Maine a world-renowned city. Thinking that this was a good idea, I put some creative juices that way. I started thinking about other 'mother stories' (and idiosyncrasies), and realized there was a prominent orange theme. My mother's *least* favorite candy in the whole world is circus peanuts. (As a joke, my brother sends some to her now and then.) Hmm...they're orange. She lives in Florida. Hmm...an orange-producing state. And, remember the terrorists in orange ponchos dancing in the streets of Jerusalem? Maybe, just maybe, I could make Shaynahoney, Maine the world capital of orange manufactured products and find a way to weave the idea of going there into our trip.

About a week before we left on our trip, my mother called to see if I had a jacket to take to Maine since it rains quite a bit there. I said that I didn't, and she told me, "Well, there's a store near me that has rain ponchos on sale. Would you like me to pick one up for you?"

I answered, "Yes, but only if it's orange." If she had been able to see me, as opposed to just hear me over the telephone, she'd have seen me wink. Maybe she'd have understood my attempt at sarcasm.

Ah, but she didn't. She replied, "OK, honey, I'll get you an orange rain poncho for our trip. Is there another color that would work for you besides orange?" Obviously, the dancing terrorists event was not prominent in her memory. Who knows, maybe rain ponchos are different than dancing terrorist ponchos.

"No," I said. "They'll have an orange one for me, I'm sure. If they don't, that's OK. Don't get me one then, because I only want orange."

"OK," she replied. "Orange it is."

After the conversation, I rubbed my hands together greedily, as if ready to plunge into a juicy steak. I was sure I could pull off my joke. I just had to buy some supplies for the trip. Nothing to do with the trip itself, mind you. Just stuff for the practical joke.

So, I wandered around Anderson's General Store in Toledo, searching the aisles for orange-colored products. I found orange ponchos, and purchased two. I found circus peanuts, orange Tic Tacs, and other orange items. I had my supplies—now I had to finalize my plan.

My thought was to type up a description of Shaynahoney, Maine. I figured I could insert it into one of our travel books and have her read about it one day on the trip. So, here's what I came up with:

Shaynahoney, Maine Area

You thought Florida was the orange capital of the world? Hardly! One of Maine's best-kept secrets is the orange capital itself—Shaynahoney.

Why is Shaynahoney known as the orange capital of the world? It is the largest manufacturer of "orange" (the color) products across the globe. What type of products come from Shaynahoney? Let's see:

Circus Peanuts
Orange Rain Ponchos
Orange Slice Candies
Orange Crush
Orange Tic Tacs
Cheese Corns
Off Mosquito Spray (in the distinctive orange can)

And their sunsets are pretty wonderful too. You don't want to miss this town. There's so much to see and buy. You'll leave thinking,…"Orange you glad you stopped in Shaynahoney, Maine!"

This promotion is brought to you by your daughter, Karen Shulman (in case you forgot), the prankster who thought you should always remember a few 'mother stories:' One, that you even thought there was a Shaynahoney, Maine. Two, that some 'mother stories' have an orange theme…circus peanuts (your complete disgust of them) and orange ponchos, you know, the dancing terrorists who wore orange ponchos in Jerusalem; the ones who turned out to be Burger Barn Restaurant umbrellas.

Actually, I never did insert it into one of our travel books. On the trip, I did most of the navigating (and got us lost—a lot), while my mom drove. So, I needed a back-up plan. At a bed and breakfast in Camden, I decided to put my note and all the orange products underneath her pillow on the bed. While she washed up one night for bed, I secretly slipped all the "goods" from my suitcase to their new hiding spot.

When she came back into the room, and started to pull the covers down on her bed, she saw the pillow was quite propped up, so she picked it up. She totally disregarded the note, and saw the orange poncho. She said excitedly, "Look! They're so nice here in Camden. They must know it rains a lot. I got a poncho under my pillow. Oh, and look, underneath the poncho there's…circus peanuts? Did you get anything under your pillow, Karen?"

I could hardly keep a straight face. "I don't think I got any goodies, Ma. But, hey, did they leave you a note with the gifts?"

"Why yes they did. Let me read it." She headed over to a chair for better lighting and read out loud: "Shaynahoney, Maine Area. You thought Florida was the orange capital of the world? HARDLY! One of Maine's best kept secrets is the orange capital itself—Shaynahoney." Well, she started laughing almost immediately as she read aloud. She finally realized she'd been had.

6

Matters of Mothering

Some of my favorite 'mother stories' have occurred when my mom has been in the act of trying to protect or educate me, or just give me good old-fashioned motherly advice. In her typical fashion, sometimes her actions don't quite come across the way they were intended. Read these mother stories to see what I mean.

It was a late Sunday afternoon in the early 1970s, and everyone was home doing his or her own thing. My mom was sewing, my dad napping on the couch; my brother was in his bedroom drawing, and I was outside shooting baskets. It was getting close to dinnertime, so my mom decided to head downstairs to the kitchen to start preparing supper. She put some oil in a pot to heat up French fries, turned on the burner and put the pot on the stove. Then, for some unknown reason, she went back upstairs to continue her sewing.

Minutes later, I came in from outside, and my brother came downstairs to see if we could snack on something before dinner. My brother walked into the kitchen and saw the pot of oil in flames on the stove. He yelled for help. My dad woke up and ran into the kitchen; my mom came flying down the stairs and raced into the kitchen. Me, I just observed; I was the littlest and felt the least helpful in this adult crisis.

My dad grabbed the pot off the stove, while my mother yelled her typical danger warning when handling something heated, "HOT! HOT! HOT!" That was the same warning I'd heard as a five-year-old, when I was anxious to find out what was for dinner one night. I decided to look inside all the pots on the stove, so proud of myself for being able to stand on my tiptoes, lift the lids up, and see what was cooking. I heard the "HOT! HOT! HOT!" warning then, too, but I wasn't all that proficient in mother-speak. As a result, I burned my right forearm by leaning on one of the pots as I attempted to see what was cooking on the back burners. Over the years, we all had learned that Ma's screams of "HOT! HOT! HOT!" were short for, "Be careful. You're getting dangerously close to burning the skin off your body!"

That evening, the warning didn't help my dad much either; he singed his arm in the flames, which were getting larger by the second. Regaining his composure, he once again picked up the pot and moved it toward the sink to pour water on the pot.

My mother screamed, "NO! NO! DON'T! (We later learned this meant something like, 'don't put water on a grease fire, dear, because water makes grease fires even worse.') Somehow my father understood my mother's language that particular time, and stopped his forward motion. In doing so, he proceeded to set the kitchen curtains on fire and the flames damaged the kitchen ceiling. My brother put out the curtains by flapping a towel against them while my dad put the flaming pot on the floor.

Even though my mom couldn't speak well, she was totally in charge of the situation. "SODA!" she yelled. 'You want a drink *now*?' I thought. 'There's an emergency, Ma, and you don't even like soda!' Nobody understood that cue, so my mother went to the pantry, got the baking soda and started dumping it on the burning pot.

But the fire was an angry one. The baking soda was too little, too late. The flames in the pot just kept raging.

"OUTSIDE!" my mother yelled. I started to run outside to get away from that nasty pot, but nobody else was moving toward an exit door. Had I interpreted something wrong again? Didn't she mean everyone get out of the house, because this house is a goner? In mother-speak, somehow everyone else knew that "OUTSIDE!" meant the pot, not us. So, somebody opened the sliding glass door off of the kitchen, and my dad, once again, picked up the pot, and moved it very rapidly to the back yard. "THROW!" she shrieked, and he raced to the far edge of our patio and flung the flaming pot onto the grass.

The fire knew it had lost the battle with the Shulman clan. Its last effort was to burn a small patch of grass down to the dirt, before it finally breathed its last breath. The lawn smoked, the pot was empty, and Ma was quiet.

You've heard the term, 'ROSE'? No? Well, in mother-speak, that means 'coming out smelling like a rose.' And, my mother, even with her one-word-at-a-time communication skills, had turned a potential disaster into a sweet victory. She not only played a huge role in ensuring our house did not burn down, she also didn't have to cook a meal that night, and got her kitchen remodeled, too. In anybody's book, that's a 'ROSE'.

◆   ◆   ◆

One of the funniest 'mother stories' that I can tell you is this one, from my senior year in high school. By this time, my mother and father had divorced. My mom was back in the dating world, and was meeting some less than stellar men. In addition, all the responsibility for raising my brother and me had been placed on her shoulders. She was a frustrated person back in those days, and, honestly, who could blame her?

I was a starter on the Southfield High School girls' basketball team. I remember being a frustrated soul back then, too. I was known by my friends as having a short fuse and a potty mouth to boot. My family really didn't see that side of me; I was a quiet, respectful young lady as far as they knew.

I can remember driving somewhere with my mom, getting pissed off about a bad driver near us, and thinking myself back on the basketball court for a moment, called him a 'fuck-wad'. One did not use profanity in our family. Fearful that I was going to get my mouth washed out with soap for swearing in front of my mother, I wilted in the passenger seat of the car, awaiting a tongue lashing at least. My mother turned to me and asked, "What did you say?"

'Oh, gosh, don't make me say it again,' I thought. Geez, I was already going to get in trouble once for saying it, and now I'd get double the punishment. "What?" I asked, thinking that maybe the whole situation would just dissolve if I acted stupid.

"That was a swear word, wasn't it?" she asked. "What was it? I liked the sound of that one."

She liked the sound of that one? What? Was my hearing playing a trick on me? Shouldn't she be yelling at me, rather than giving me some sign of approval for my foul use of the English language? Finally, I dared to answer, "Umm, Ma, the word was 'fuck-wad.'"

"Does it have a meaning?" she asked.

"No, I don't think so. It's just a name you call somebody who pisses you off," I explained. I then thought to myself, this is too good to be true. Now I'm going to get the real message, the real anger, and the real punishment for saying a cuss word. I cringed a little more in anticipation.

"Can you teach me other words like that one? Sometimes I want to swear when I get angry, but I just don't know the words," she explained.

I finally relaxed. This was going to be just fine, after all. For the next half hour or so, I proceeded to give my mother a lesson in how to swear. Never in my life would I have anticipated that particular scene with my mother. Oh, but the story doesn't end there.

Let's go back to the basketball season of my senior year. We were getting close to the end of the season. Our arch rival that year was Ferndale High School. Ferndale's team was tall (really tall), and strong (really strong), and fast (really fast). They always put together a good team. We had already played once at Ferndale and lost. In fact, a Southfield High girls' basketball team had never beaten a Ferndale High team, until one particular fall night in 1978, when the two teams were playing each other at the Southfield High School gym.

My mom was at that game, and it was a real nail-biter. It was a back and forth battle that came down to the last seconds of the game. We had just scored a bucket and with fifteen seconds left, were behind by a point. Ferndale was taking the ball out of bounds under our basket, as we applied some pressure defense. They in-bounded the ball safely, made another pass, and out of nowhere, our guard intercepted the pass, raced the half court, and made a lay-up at the buzzer. Southfield High School had beaten the mighty Ferndale team and pandemonium had broken out in our gym. We were smiling and yelling and jumping and whooping it up any which way we could, because we had just made history!

A while later, leaving the school, I walked with my mom to our car. To celebrate our victory, the whole team, and any spectators who wanted to join us, were going out for a bite to eat. As we walked to the car, the Ferndale High School bus, with its deflated girls' basketball team in it, passed by us. The windows were rolled down and some of the players had their heads sticking out in the cool air. One of their players shouted "Southfield Sucks! Southfield Sucks!"

Granted, that made me mad, but I figured I'd feel the same way if I were in their shoes, so I ignored the words and proceeded to the car. Not my mother. Before I could stop her, she was off and running, arms flailing, toward the bus yelling, "Well, Ferndale fucks! Ferndale fucks, you little fuck-wads!" Angered, she just kept running after the departing bus, repeating her message.

Have you ever felt there was an appropriate time for a role reversal with a parent? Well, this was my time. I knew that if I didn't stop her soon, we were going to be involved in something rather ugly. I ran after her and dragged her back to the car. I placed her in the driver seat, slammed the door, walked to my side of the car, and got in. We got into the car and I yelled at her, "What are you doing? Are you trying to get us killed?"

"You girls are nice girls, and you deserved to win that game. You don't suck, and you don't deserve to be told you do. They pissed me off. I just used the words you taught me. How did I do?"

Just then, I said words I thought I'd never say to my mother. "Your actions tonight show that you can't handle swear words. I have created a monster! So, there will be no more lessons in how to swear for you. From now on, Ma, you're cut off!" At that moment, I realized that parenting, especially of your own parent, is a tough job.

In case you were wondering, she *has* sworn since then, and done so many times, I'm sure. But from that day on, she never learned another swear word directly from *me*.

◆   ◆   ◆

These next two stories have made me wonder over the years if my mother really gave birth to me, and if she really understood me at all. Or perhaps they're just cases of her saying things that came to mind and that might have been better left unsaid.

As a kid I was not a clotheshorse, nor did I like to shop for clothing. It was exhausting and tedious, and I just hated the *thought* of going shopping, let alone actually doing it. Despite my protests, my mother dragged me out to the store one day to shop for clothes, and, in a typical teen-age fashion, wanting her to know I did not want to be there, I was grumpy and not all that cooperative. She ignored me.

"Try this on," she said, holding up something hideous. "Oh, this is cute. This would look good on you. Try it on, OK?"

"Ugh!" I answered. "I hate it."

"Try it on anyway, dear. It might look better on *you* than the hanger," she said patiently.

"Alright," I huffed. Then I tried on the clothes, praying they'd be as ugly on me as they were on the hanger. So far that day, my prayers had been answered. Nothing fit and nothing looked good.

This scenario went on for what seemed like several hours. She'd find 'cute' things for me to try on. I'd hate them and put them on begrudgingly. Nothing fit or looked all that well.

Determined, my mom decided to give it one last try. She was at one rack of clothes, while I looked less than half-heartedly at another rack. She called over to me and said, "Karen. I found something you're bound to like. Come here and look at this top. It's big, ugly, and sloppy looking."

Something else you should know about me is that I really like good food. I love to go out to eat, especially with friends. I particularly like places with short waits to get seated, large portions of great tasting food, and a comfortable, smoke free, semi-quiet environment so that I can hear and participate in conversation.

One night, my mom, Sam, my brother, and I were going out to dinner at a popular restaurant in Walled Lake. We passed by several nice lake homes and pretty lakefront property on our way there. As we passed by another restaurant called the Wayside Inn, my mom turned to the back seat to ask me a question. "Have you ever been to that restaurant, Karen?"

"The Wayside Inn?" I asked. "No, Ma, I've never been there. Why?"

"Well, you'd like it. It's smoky, loud, crowded, and the food's not very good," she answered.

"Ma, what in that description would make you think I'd like to eat in a place like that?" I returned.

"Oh, now that I think about it, nothing. Hmm…never mind."

◆   ◆   ◆

It certainly is a mother's prerogative to worry about her children. And over the years, my mother has done more than her fair share of worrying, in her own special way. This story is a classic example of how worrying can make my mother put two and two together and not even come close to four.

After I moved from our Detroit-area home to Toledo, Ohio, my folks and I would meet periodically for dinner in Ann Arbor, roughly the half-way point. We had scheduled to meet one night at five-o'clock sharp, at a restaurant called The Fish House. I knew my way around Ann Arbor somewhat, although I'd never been to The Fish House. So, I decided to go up to Ann Arbor a bit early in order to find the restaurant. It was easier to find than I had anticipated. I still had about twenty minutes to kill before my folks arrived. Driving around Ann Arbor seemed to be a good way to kill time, so I drove around and wound up getting lost.

It was after 5 p.m., and I knew my mother was going to panic. Having been trained by her to be prompt—always—I'm usually right on time or on the early side. Not that night. By the time I found my way back to the restaurant, it was twenty minutes past five.

The hostess took me to the booth where my mom and Sam were waiting. He looked happy and cheerful, while my mother looked like she had just seen a ghost. She let out a huge sigh of relief as I slid into my side of the booth. "Is

everything OK?" I asked. "I'm sorry I'm late. I *was* here early but drove around to kill time and wound up getting lost."

My mother was so out of sorts that she couldn't speak. Sam started laughing, and I was just confused. 'She's ashen white, and he's laughing,' I thought. 'What is going on?'

Through his laughter, Sam explained that there were a few fish items that were on the menu but not available that night for dinner—red snapper, scrod, and monkfish. He hoped I didn't want any of those choices. He further explained that those items were not available because the truck delivering the fish had been in an accident on the way to the restaurant.

"So why are you laughing, and why does mom look petrified?" I asked.

"Your mother is the funniest woman I've ever met. She was convinced that the reason you were late was because you had an accident with the fish truck!"

◆   ◆   ◆

My dad's mom (we lovingly called her Honey Doris) lived in Florida for the last twenty years of her life. She and my grandfather (Honey Ted) made a wonderful home for themselves down south after my Dad passed away.

Honey Ted lived to be ninety-four; he was a kind, gentle man who was full of love. Honey Doris lived a few more years after he passed. Though only four-feet-eleven-inches tall, she was a self-proclaimed "feisty broad", an independent woman who took guff from no one, and who was determined to live to be 120.

But by 1999, Honey Doris' health had started to decline. Despite health issues, she still insisted on driving ("like a bat out of hell"), shopping daily, and paying her own bills. Believe it or not, she really was a pretty decent driver at the age of ninety-three, and she kept her financial records and important papers better than younger people I knew (including me). It took a lot to slow her down. She was hospitalized a few times during 1999 and hated every minute; the hospital was "full of old people," and she couldn't wait to get out of there and go on with her life. In October of that year, she developed an intense case of shingles (her immune system had totally shut down), and she grew very weak. Her doctors called to tell me that there was nothing more they could do for her. They suggested that I come down to Florida during the next few days, to sign the paperwork needed to put her in Hospice.

This was on a Wednesday. I called Spirit Airlines immediately to get a flight out that Friday; they booked me for a 7 a.m. flight out of Detroit. Why did I wait to travel until Friday? I don't remember the particulars. Probably based on my schedule, I had things I could not easily reschedule. In reality, somebody was watching over me. The east coast of Florida was slammed with a hurricane that Thursday. Having never wanted to be a hurricane flight warrior, it's a good thing I skipped that day for flying.

I kept calling Spirit Airlines Thursday night to see if they were flying on Friday, and they kept saying all flights for Friday were still on. I got up extra early (about 3 a.m.) Friday morning to call Spirit again. All flights were still a go. I left my house by 4:15 and drove up to Detroit.

Arriving at the airport an hour and a half before flight time (like a good passenger), I was tired and couldn't wait to get to the gate area and close my eyes. I had about an hour before boarding would start, so I relaxed, and tried to catch a few winks, but suddenly I heard my name over the loudspeaker. "Karen Shulman, please come to the ticketing counter; we have a message for you."

I was sure I must be in la-la-land and was only dreaming about my name being paged. So, I drifted back to a relaxed state. Then I heard it again, "Karen Shulman, please come to the ticketing counter; we have a message for you."

Now I was awake. Had I left my trunk open or the lights on in my car? Had I forgotten something back home? God forbid, had my grandmother already passed? I rushed to the check-in booth and told them I was Karen Shulman.

"Your mother called. She said, 'don't come,'" explained the Spirit Airlines attendant.

"Don't come?" I asked in my half-stupor.

"Your mother called and said, 'don't come'. They have no electrical power," she explained.

I then inquired, "Is my mother still on the phone?"

"No, honey. She hung up," was the attendant's answer.

I was feeling very awake by now. Who in the world would call an airline and leave a message for a passenger, waiting to board a flight within minutes, telling them, "Don't come"?

My mother, that's who!

"Do you have a phone I can use to call her back?" I asked.

"No, but there's a pay phone right down the hall. You're welcome to use that," the attendant offered.

Terrific. How very helpful. The attendant and my mother must have agreed it would be fun to terrorize me at 6 a.m. The following is what I remember doing and thinking as I tried to reach my mother before my flight left for Florida:

I took inventory of the resources I had, which were bupkus (that's 'nothing' in Yiddish). I had no cell phone, no calling card, and no change. Well, there was always collect calling. I ran to a pay phone and dialed my mother's number. It just rang and rang and rang. They had no power and, in this case, no phone service, either.

Next I tried to place a collect call to my mother's cell phone, but this second attempt at collect calling worked no better than the first. An operator came on the line and told me that collect calls to cell phones were not allowed.

I explained my predicament to the operator. "Can I charge the call to my home phone?" I asked.

In her sweet operator voice she replied, "Is there someone home who can take the call, dear, to verify that you are who you say you are?"

"Uh…NO…I'm here at the Detroit airport making this call, so I'm not at home right now to verify who I am, now *am* I, dear?" I said sarcastically, beginning to lose my patience.

I had another idea, but I needed this woman on my side. Attempting to smooth things over, I asked politely, "Can I charge the call to my credit card?"

"No, dear. We don't do that, unless you have one of *our* credit cards," she explained.

"No." I told her, "We've struck out on that, too. Go figure; I have a credit card that earns me flight miles, not free phone time. Help me out here, please. I have run out of ideas. Is there some way I can make this call, because *I have* to make this call?" I pleaded.

The operator went into telephone employee mode. "It will cost you $4.25 for a three minute phone call. You will need the $4.25 in change, not bills."

'No shit, Sherlock!' I thought to myself. 'Even I know there's no slot in pay phones for dollar bills,' although with those prices, I believed there should be. "OK," I said, "I'll go see if I can get some change. Thanks for your help," and I was off and running to the nearby magazine stand.

Running up to the cashier, I told my story while trying to catch my breath. He explained that he wasn't supposed to make change, but he'd give me two dollars worth since he felt this was an emergency. Handing him two one-dollar bills, I thanked him several times, then went running to the food stand across the hall.

"We are not allowed to give change," smiled the clerk behind the counter, in answer to my explanation and plea for help. "But, if you buy something, we can give you change back."

Finally, the last bit of help I needed was here. I explained my plan to the cashier. "OK, charge me for the cheapest thing on your menu, and don't give it to me. I don't want a pop or a donut or anything. Here's my money. Just please give me the change in coins, if you can."

I left the food counter and magazine stand with about $4.50 in change. It was a good thing I didn't have to go through another metal detector. I'd have been pulled over for setting it off and for having a pile of change in my pocket big enough to look like a weapon.

Running back to the pay phone, I dialed my mom's cell phone. She answered, and I started talking quickly. "Ma, this is Karen. We have to make this fast, OK? The plane is going to board soon, and I only have so much change for this call. I got your message at the airport. What did you mean by, 'Don't come?'"

"It's a mess here. We had a hurricane yesterday. Why is Spirit Airlines even flying here? Do they know we had a hurricane yesterday?" she replied in her typical fashion.

I tried to remain calm, but she hadn't really answered my question. I was pressured for time, and I started to get angry. "MA!" I shouted. "Spirit is flying and I'm guessing they're more than aware that you had a hurricane yesterday. Listen to me. Why should I not come?"

She must have really concentrated on what I asked this time. She replied, "We have water, high water, all over, and it's flooded the streets. We were the center of the hurricane, you know. The water's so high that we can't pick you up at the airport. We can't get out of our development. And, we have no power. You'll be uncomfortable here."

'I'll be uncomfortable there?' I thought. In her panic over the hurricane, she lost sight of the purpose for my visit. So I helped her refocus. "Ma, I'm already at the airport. I've been here since 5:30 a.m. I'm coming down to Florida today. Honey Doris needs to be put in Hospice care. I don't care if you can't pick me up. I'll rent something at the airport if you are not there to greet me, OK?"

"Well you'd better rent something high off the ground. The water is three feet high in our development alone. I'm telling you, there are cars buried in water here. I really don't think you should come. The driving is awful, and I think you should stay home," she pleaded her case.

I looked up to see the gate area for my flight emptying, as people began boarding the plane. "OK, Ma. I hear you, but I'm coming anyway. If I see you at the airport, great. If not, I'll rent a vehicle. They're boarding my flight now. I have to go. Oh, one more thing. You have three hours to mop up your development before I get there, so get busy, OK? I love you. Bye."

I ran back to the gate and got on my flight. In a few hours, I was in Florida. My folks were there to greet me. They had borrowed their next-door neighbor's SUV. We wound up renting a van for our use, since the SUV needed to be returned.

Was my mother exaggerating about the water? No she wasn't, not in the least. There were cars buried in water, traffic lights out, intersections closed, and roads completely flooded. (Obviously, her mopping up while I flew was insufficient to make a dent in the water levels.)

Thankfully, I was able to drive carefully and, most importantly, to take care of my grandmother's needs. I'm glad I ignored my mother's order, "Don't come!" And, I figured out who the hurricane flight worrier (versus warrior) was in the family.

◆   ◆   ◆

This story is a matter of mothering if you recall that my divorced mother was trying to find a new life partner and surrogate father for her children. A few pages back, I told you point blank that my mother was dating less than stellar men. Well, one day my mother 'woke up' and realized she needed a huge improvement in the 'men I'm dating' department.

"Karen," she said to me one morning. "When you go to school, sometime this week, could you talk to Fred Goldberg, your athletic director, and ask him if he knows any nice men for me to date?"

YES! My prayers had been answered. She finally recognized that the guys she'd been dating were a bunch of…less than desirable? Idiots? OK, just plain creeps. Now, another person may have been thrown off by being asked to consult with the athletic director. That's not who I'd call the typical person you'd go to for matchmaking. But I knew Mr. Goldberg, and I knew why she had targeted him, because I know my mother. Fred Goldberg was a Jewish man, a little older than she, and so she figured he must know some nice, single Jewish, men. I certainly hoped she was right.

"Sure, Mom. I'll talk to Mr. Goldberg when I get a chance. I'll let you know what he says," I answered, as coolly as I could.

The minute I got to school that very same day, I ran to Mr. Goldberg's office to inquire. "Mr. Goldberg, I have a very important question for you. You know my mom's been divorced for a few years now, right?"

"Sure, honey. I know," he answered.

"And, do you know that my mother is dating some creeps—I mean, do you know that she could be dating better men?" I asked trying to be more positive (after all, I had to make the sale).

"Sure, honey. I know," he answered.

He wasn't as enthused as I wanted him to be. Honestly, I wasn't even sure he was listening. I was afraid I was losing him. He was a busy guy; I figured I'd better get to the point. "Well, do you know any nice, single men for my mother to date?" I finally asked.

Freddie stopped and thought for a minute. "You girls have a home basketball game this Thursday, right?"

"Yes we do," I replied.

"Hmm…I think Sammy is refereeing your game this Thursday. Do you have a minute, honey? I'll find out for sure," he offered.

I nodded yes as if I wasn't about to be late for class, and had all the time in the world to handle this most important issue. Mr. Goldberg picked up the phone and dialed a number. "Sammy, this is Molly," Mr. Goldberg started the conversation.

Now I was confused. Molly? Who the hell was Molly? His name was Fred or Freddie, not Molly. What the heck, I figured I'd let that go and just continue to listen.

"You have our girls' varsity game this Thursday, right? Good. What are you doing after the game? Nothing? Good. Good. Hold on a minute," He looked at me and put his hand over the receiver.

"Is your mom coming to the game this Thursday, Karen?" he asked.

"Yes, she's coming," I answered.

Now he showed some enthusiasm. "Sammy, there's a girl that plays on our team. Her mom is single, smart, funny, and attractive, very attractive. You'll love her. She's great. How about you, me, Micki—that's our player's mom—how about we go out for drinks and a bite to eat after the game? Good. Great. O.K. I've got to go. See you Thursday," he said and then hung up the phone.

I was thrilled. I believed he had just made a date for my mom. "Well?" I asked.

"Go home and tell your mom that she has to come to the game on Thursday, and that she has a date for drinks and dinner after the game. Tell her I'm going, too, so that she's comfortable meeting Sam," he explained.

"Sam, the referee?" I asked. "Is he the short, dark-haired, bowlegged guy that we had ref some of our games the past few years?" I inquired. Why I remembered him, I don't know for sure. I think when he'd refereed an earlier game of ours, I thought he looked Jewish and was amazed, because refereeing was not a common profession for a Jewish person, and I certainly remembered his bowleggedness.

"He's the one. He's a nice man, and I think the two of them will hit it off. Make sure your mom comes to the game, OK?" he told me.

Well, they went out that Thursday night as planned. And, they *must* have hit it off, and Sam *must* have been a nice man. They were married the next year, and have been married ever since.

What are the morals of this story? First, always listen to your mother when she wants to dump the losers and tells you to ask others about nice, single men for her to date. Second, don't exclude Athletic Directors (especially ones named Molly Goldberg) as matchmakers.

7

The Kindergarten Teacher

Before my mother retired, she was a kindergarten teacher. The kids just loved her. She was sweet, kind, pretty, and funny (as we've seen), and she was a great teacher. Not all the funny things that happened in my mom's classroom were just related to her, however. The kids played a huge role in many funny 'mother stories.' Here are samples of some of those stories:

My mom knew the importance of family in the development (or lack thereof) of young children. She tried to bring teaching tools into her classroom that would help with understanding families of all kinds. One way she tried to impart knowledge about family was keeping a cage of live gerbils in her classroom. Kids were able to see the animals eat, drink, play, take care of babies, give birth, give birth, give birth, and give birth some more. (Have you ever been around gerbils? You get to watch them give birth quite frequently.) My mom's students were allowed to play with them only by holding or petting them within the cage. On one particular day, my mom walked by a group of students huddling around the gerbil cage. One little girl was holding the mommy gerbil in one hand and the daddy gerbil in the other. My mom heard the little girl talking to the gerbils, telling them things about their roles as mommy and daddy. At one point, with intense concentration, the student exclaimed, "Kiss, Kiss, Kiss!" while she pushed (smacked) the mommy and daddy gerbils' mouths together each time she repeated the word 'Kiss'.

'Susie is obviously making a family connection with the gerbils,' my mother thought to herself, and she chuckled. She then called the class together for story time; so all other play activities ceased, including gerbil playtime. Later that afternoon, after the students had gone home, my mom realized that gerbil playtime had really ceased. In her zeal to have the mommy and daddy gerbil kiss, the little girl had accidentally broken the mommy gerbil's neck. The next day, the kids also learned about gerbil heaven.

◆   ◆   ◆

Remember milk and cookie time in kindergarten? My mom's classroom was a typical kindergarten where milk and cookies were part of the daily routine, and there were certain rules to be followed regarding milk and cookie time. Nobody was allowed to take more than one treat, unless there were some left after everyone had firsts. The kids knew they had to be polite and thank the person that brought in the treats. They also knew that when they finished, any paper products had to be thrown away and any leftover milk had to be poured into a silver bucket. "Why?" you ask. Good question. I wondered that myself. To avoid having milk get warm, spoil, and smell up class wastebaskets, the janitor would pick up the unused milk (in the silver bucket) and pour it down a drain. Pretty smart thinking, I'd say.

One day, little Johnny was having great fun running around the classroom after milk and cookie time (he must have been on a very intense sugar buzz). He wasn't looking where he was going, and he accidentally kicked over the full silver bucket. Milk spilled and splashed everywhere. Upset that he'd made a mess, Johnny started to cry.

My mother, teacher, nurturer and humorist, was there to make him feel better. "Don't worry, Johnny," she said. "There's no use crying over spilt milk." She was so proud of herself for saying something funny to comfort one of her students in an upsetting moment.

But when she looked up she saw nobody was laughing. You see, Mom forgot one of the key rules about public speaking—know your audience. One of the unfortunate things about teaching five-year-olds is that not all of your spectators fully grasp the concept of everything you're saying.

◆   ◆   ◆

Supernatural ability was not something my mother cultivated in her kindergarten students, but one of my mom's students turned out to be a psychic of sorts.

When my mother returned to her classroom after lunch one afternoon, one of her bright pupils, Billy, told her, "Mrs. Shulman, I know what you had for lunch today."

"You do, Billy?" my mother replied in a surprised tone.

"I do!" he answered excitedly.

She wondered how he knew what she ate. Was he at the restaurant where she had eaten? No, the restaurant was very small, and she didn't see him there. Billy had certainly piqued her interest. "OK, Billy. What did I have for lunch?" she asked.

"You had tuna fish, Mrs. Shulman. Am I right? Am I right?"

My mother was in shock. She *had*, in fact, had tuna fish that day for lunch. 'How in the world did Billy know?' she wondered. Could it be he smelled her breath? No, she was too far away from Billy for him to get a whiff of tuna breath. Was he psychic? She was stumped, so she decided to ask. "You are right, Billy! How did you know I had tuna fish for lunch?"

"You know the glasses that you have around your neck? Well, Mrs. Shulman, there is a glob of tuna fish on them," explained Billy.

It's a good thing he was "psychic" or just had wonderful eyesight. My mom could have easily wound up with tuna fish in her eye when she put on her glasses that afternoon, and that would have been a whole 'nother 'mother story.'

◆   ◆   ◆

Teaching kindergarten, my mom was able to explore lots of different subjects. She taught generations of kids about apples, butterflies, words, animals, letters, numbers, stories, painting, holidays, and even some history. One year, while talking about Presidents' Day, she taught the kids all about Abraham Lincoln. She told them about his hard work and the dedication it took him to become President of the United States. She also told them about some of the things he accomplished in office. The students also learned about the unfortunate end to his life. They read stories about him, drew pictures of him, and even made tall hats (like he wore) out of construction paper.

A few months after that lesson, the school building where my mother taught was put up for sale. There were frequent visitors touring and inspecting the school for possible purchase. One day, my mom's class was lined up in the hallway to go outside for recess. As they waited anxiously to go outside, one of the prospective buyers passed the kids in the hall. He was a rabbi, tall and bearded, dressed all in black, and wearing a tall, black hat.

One of my mom's students shot her hand up in the air with a question as soon as she eyed the man. She followed him with her gaze as he walked down the hallway.

"Yes, Cathy. You have a question," said my mother.

"Mrs. Shulman. I thought you told us that Abe Lincoln was dead."

8

Could It Be Hereditary?

I've asked myself many times, what makes my mother so amusing without even trying to be, and where does this talent come from? Even more importantly, will I be the same way? Well, an honest look into these questions has made me realize that heredity must play a role. Let me share with you some stories about my grandmother (Honey Anne) and me that will help illustrate that there is probably some gene for funniness that has been passed on through three generations.

Grandmother (Honey Anne) Stories

Like my mother, Honey Anne can be fun to travel with. Back in the 1970s, our family took a three-week vacation to Europe. My mom, dad, brother, and I toured parts of Germany and Italy and then went on to Israel. Later, both sets of grandparents—Honey Doris and Honey Ted (my dad's folks) and Honey Anne and Honey Joe (my mom's folks) met us in Israel. It was there that I got a glimpse into why my mother sometimes talks the way she does.

One very hot afternoon, after we had been touring all morning, we stopped at a roadside stand to get some sodas and other refreshments. Since Honey Anne had never been a soda pop drinker, she asked the clerk if they had any orange juice.

"Yes, ma'am, we do," answered the boy, in a thick Israeli accent.

"Does it come freshly squozen?" she asked.

Even those of us that spoke English knew that "squozen" wasn't an English word. Of course, my mother totally understood what my grandmother was asking. So did I. The Israeli boy at the stand, however, was clueless.

◆　　　◆　　　◆

Honey Anne has been a pretty hip woman for most of her adult life. She has always looked great, dressed beautifully, and kept up with the latest fashion trends. She has always been active. She has been a long-time volunteer for a number of organizations, worked for many charitable causes, taken classes, exercised, traveled, spent lots of time with family, and been very active in her synagogue.

When my grandfather (Honey Joe) was nearing retirement, my grandparents decided to buy a condominium in Florida. They chose to spend most of their winters in Florida, and spent the rest of the seasons in Michigan. I used to visit them in Florida, often during my winter breaks from school.

My grandmother was probably even more active than usual during her winter months in Florida. She'd take art classes, dance lessons, play cards, cook, and entertain. Once, she even took belly-dancing lessons at her condominium complex.

One evening, she was in her kitchen making dinner. As she cooked, she practiced some of her belly-dancing moves. The phone rang, and she answered the call. "Is this the swinger?" asked a man's voice on the other end.

She didn't exactly recognize the voice and wondered which neighbor had been watching her practice her dancing. Surely it was someone with binoculars. She figured she must be pretty good, too, since they were referring to her as 'the swinger.' As she swayed her hips from side to side she answered, "It sure is!"

The man then said, "Great! I'd like to make a reservation for two tonight at nine-o'clock."

My grandmother was now very confused. "The swinger? Reservations? I'm not sure I understand," she replied.

"Is this _____?" he recited a phone number.

"No. You're close. It's _____." She told him he was off by one number.

"Oh," he said a bit embarrassed. "I must have the wrong number. I thought I had dialed The Swinger Nightclub at the Floridian Grand Hotel. Sorry for your trouble."

My grandmother laughed and hung up the phone. Unlike my mother, she knew when someone had truly dialed a wrong number.

◆   ◆   ◆

Several years later, my grandmother moved into a new condominium, one that was closer to family, and offered lots of activities. Her condo was in an eight-story high rise, and she lived on the third floor.

One day, she noticed that her kitchen ceiling was leaking. She called maintenance to see if they could send somebody over to help. (That's common in our family; if something breaks, we call somebody else to do the repairs. We are *not* mechanically inclined.) A short while later, a maintenance man knocked on her door. He came into the kitchen and checked all around. He went out on her porch and checked there as well. He looked at the ceilings throughout her condo and still wasn't sure what was causing the problem. "I'm going to go check the gutters. I'll be right back," he said.

She let him out of her condo and sat down to think about what he had said. She had never considered herself very knowledgeable about building construction and she was baffled. Why would gutters on the roof of an eight-story building cause her third floor ceiling to leak? It just didn't make any sense. She racked her brain some more, but the more she thought about it, the more mystified she got.

Soon there was a knock at the door. The maintenance man had returned. "Sure enough, it was a problem with the gutters. The leak should be stopping real soon," he explained.

"That's nice. I have a question though. Could you explain to me how gutters on the roof of this eight story building could cause *my* kitchen ceiling to leak?" she asked.

"Not the gutters on the roof of the building," he said between laughs. "The neighbors right above you. You know. The Gutters. Their dishwasher had a leak and the overflow came through your kitchen ceiling."

"Now that makes more sense!" she exclaimed, laughing.

◆ ◆ ◆

When I'm not jotting down 'mother stories,' I work as a massage therapist. Several years ago, while I was still in massage therapy school, I drove up to Michigan to give my grandmother a massage. I got her all set up on my table, turned on some nice soft instrumental music, and started the massage. I worked her head and face first, and then moved to her right arm and hand. Her skin was incredibly soft, unbelievably soft for a seventy-five-year-old woman. I asked her how she kept it so soft, and she said she didn't know. I asked her if she used a lot of moisturizers and things, but she said no. She explained that daily baths with bath beads were probably helpful in keeping her skin soft.

I was truly amazed. I told her that I'd massaged twenty-year-olds with skin not nearly as soft as hers.

I continued with the massage, working her chest, left arm and hand, neck and shoulders and then on to the left leg. "How did you get so many bruises, Honey Anne? Your left arm and leg have lots of bruising," I explained.

"I don't know, Karen. I think I'm getting wider," she answered.

I started to laugh. "You think you're getting wider? What do you mean?"

"I don't know. I must be eating too much and getting wider. Every time I enter or leave a room through a doorway, I knock myself. So, I figure I must be getting wider," she offered.

I thought about her explanation for a minute. If she were getting wider, which I didn't think was the case, wouldn't she have bruising on *both* sides? Then I looked up at her face, and I found my answer. I remembered about the procedure she had just undergone not too long before. "Honey Anne?" I said with a questioning tone. "Didn't you just have cataract surgery done, and wasn't that done on your left eye?"

"Yes. Yes. I did. Well, I guess I'm not getting wider after all," she said with relief.

In our family (my mother with her mastectomy and my grandmother with her cataract treatment, for example), we must tend to forget about recent surgical procedures and how they impact our daily lives.

◆   ◆   ◆

Honey Anne is one of the biggest fans of the color pink that you could ever meet. She likes pink in all shades. Her condo in Michigan had hot pink Formica kitchen counter tops, and one of her bathrooms had velvety-cranberry colored wallpaper with swashes of silver. There were pink paintings, pink linens, pink tablecloths, pink rugs, and pink dishes, too. I know it sounds wild, but it really was very beautiful. My friends dubbed her place The Pink Palace, and it fit. Heck, there was a time when the only color my grandmother wore was pink.

Another fact that you should know about my grandmother is that she loves music. She plays the piano like an absolute pro. She's the life of any party where there's a piano to play and people to sing along. Amazingly, she plays by ear—she never learned to read musical notes.

A few years ago, my grandmother went into a dollar store in Florida and found a scarf that seemed made just for her. It was white and hot pink, and the print of the material had a musical notes and pianos motif. She just had to have it, and so she bought it. What a bargain for a buck!

The next Sunday, when her sisters and brother-in-law, my folks, and one of my aunts got together for breakfast, she wore her new scarf and encouraged everyone to look at it. Everyone told her how beautiful it looked on her.

Once seated at a table, my grandmother asked again if everyone liked her scarf. "Yes," they replied. After all, they'd all ooooooo' d and ahhhhhh'd over it just minutes before.

"Well, would anyone like my scarf? I don't want it," she declared.

"Mother, why wouldn't you want the scarf?" asked my mom. "It's absolutely perfect for you. It's your color and it has pianos and musical notes on it. What's wrong with it?"

"It has writing on it. I never saw the writing on it in the store. I must have been too excited about the music and the color. Look at what it says! I don't want it!" she exclaimed.

My mother looked more closely at the scarf. Written all over the print of the scarf was 'I love Jesus and Jesus loves me.' Perhaps this was not the most perfect scarf after all, for my Jewish grandmother. Perhaps this was also a deeper look into our family's visual challenges.

The story doesn't end there. After all, I can be a practical joker, and why play all my practical jokes on my mother? Surely one was called for here.

I thought it would be really funny if I could find a matching bracelet for my grandmother's scarf, and I had the perfect bracelet in mind. If only I could find it in pink. I went to four different stores and finally was able to find what I was looking for in cranberry; not exactly pink, but close enough.

My family was getting together for dinner to celebrate my grandmother's eighty-fifth birthday. She had just returned from wintering in Florida, so, for many of us, it was to be our first visit with her since arriving home. In addition to my grandmother, my brother, aunts, uncles, and cousins were going to be there. Perfect! I'd have an audience for my practical joke. I called my grandmother and asked if she'd brought her new scarf back from Florida.

"What scarf?" she barked.

"The Jesus scarf," I answered.

"Oh, that scarf," she said with slight embarrassment. Quickly recovering, she offered, "You want it? Does one of your friends want it? I don't want it," she said.

"No, Honey Anne, I don't want it, and I don't think any of my friends will want it. What I wanted to know was if you would bring it today to Aunt Joanie and Uncle Paul's. I'd like to see it, OK?" I said.

"Sure, honey. I'll bring it for you. And you take it home, OK? I don't want it. Really!" she finished.

"I'll see you in a couple of hours, OK? And, don't forget to bring the scarf." With that, I hung up and got ready to head up to Michigan.

Dinner with the family was great. We relish the times we're together, because they don't happen all that frequently anymore. And celebrating a grandmother's eighty-fifth birthday doesn't happen every day, either.

After dinner, we surrounded my grandmother as she opened gifts. When she had finished, I announced that there was one more present. "Honey Anne," I said. "Do you have the scarf I asked you to bring?"

"Yes I do!" she squealed excitedly, thinking she was finally going to be rid of the thing. She grabbed it out of her purse and thrust it at me. "Take it. It's yours!!"

"You may not want to give it to me so fast, Honey Anne. I have something to go with it, and you might want to keep it," I suggested.

"What do you have?" she asked impatiently and with a bit of distrust in her voice.

"Here, I bought you a bracelet to match. It's not an exact color match, but the theme is the same." I handed my grandmother a cranberry "WWJD" bracelet.

"What's this? What is WWJO? I can't read it. Is that what it says?" she demanded to know.

"It's WWJD, Honey Anne. It stands for What Would Jesus Do? Doesn't it go perfectly with the scarf?" I teased her.

"What would Jesus Do? Couldn't it stand for something else?" she inquired.

"How about What Would Joe Do?" I suggested. Joe was her late husband, my grandfather. She loved and honored him in life and does so to this very day.

She beamed with glee. "I like it. I'll take the bracelet. You keep the scarf." And, with that, her transaction, and my practical joke were concluded.

◆   ◆   ◆

On Rosh Hashanah-eve 2002, my grandmother had a spell where she wasn't feeling too well. While eating dinner at her sister's, she suddenly felt faint. Soon, she broke out into a sweat and was somewhat non-responsive for a while. My great-aunt and the other guests thought it would be best to call 911. They wound up taking my grandmother to the hospital where she was kept overnight for observation.

I had planned on picking up my grandmother and taking her to synagogue for the first day of Rosh Hashanah, but my great-aunt called me the night before, to tell me that my grandmother had been taken to the hospital. She told me to call the hospital in the morning and see if Honey Anne had been released before I traveled up to Michigan. I was concerned, but my great-aunt assured me that my grandmother had been doing much better by the time her visitors had left the hospital that night.

When I called the next morning, my grandmother was still there. I drove up to the hospital to spend time with her, figuring synagogue could wait for us until the next holiday. I arrived at the hospital at the same time as my Aunt Joanie, and we walked together to my grandmother's holding room in the emergency ward. My grandmother looked great. She was wearing a hospital robe and still had on her make-up and jewelry from the night before.

"The fake pearls make the outfit, Honey Anne," I said. "You look marvelous. How do you feel?"

"Oh, I feel fine. I just wish they'd let me out of here, but they're going to give me a stress test, and I can't go until they get that all done," she complained.

Just then, the nurses came in to take her for her stress test. They suggested we go to breakfast, since it would be about ninety minutes before the test would be complete. So they whisked my grandmother off, and my aunt and I left to get a bite to eat.

To make a long story short, the doctors did not like the looks of the stress test. They came in to the holding room and told my grandmother the news. My Uncle Paul and I listened to what the doctor told her. He indicated that the stress test showed an abnormality in the heart, and that she would have to be admitted. Because it was a Saturday, he also explained that no further testing or decisions would be made on her case until her doctor reported in for duty on Monday.

"But I can't stay here. I don't have my make-up or my face cleansers. I have a luncheon on Tuesday. I can't stay," she told him, matter-of-factly.

"I can't make you stay here if you don't want to. But, I wouldn't leave the hospital if I were you. I saw a large abnormality on your heart, and it would be very dangerous for you to leave right now. I would absolutely advise against your leaving here today," he explained.

"But I don't want to stay," she whined.

By this time, my uncle and I had joined forces with the doctor. She eventually agreed to stay and be admitted.

About fifteen minutes after the doctor's news, we waited in silence for Honey Anne's move to a permanent room. My grandmother was sitting on the side of the bed and started swinging her feet back and forth like a little girl. "I don't want to stay here. I don't want to stay here. SHIT! DAMMIT! I DON'T WANT TO STAY IN THIS FUCKING PLACE! GET ME OUT OF THIS SHITTY HOSPITAL! I WANT TO GO HOME!" she yelled.

I was shocked, and, judging by the look on my uncle's face, so was he. I whispered to him, "Have you ever heard her swear like that before?" He shook his head no. I wasn't sure what to say. The room had gone dead quiet. My grandmother was obviously upset, and I'd never heard her vent like that before. 'Was it possible that *I* instigated the use of profanity in my family?' I thought. The only thing I could think to contribute, in order to break the ice, was to say something, but what?

"Did I teach you that?" I asked.

"Oh no, honey. I can swear with the best of 'em when I'm angry. And right now, I'm angry. I do not want to stay here," she explained.

"Yes, Honey Anne. You've made that abundantly clear," I answered.

That broke the tension, and we all laughed. To everyone's relief, she was released from the hospital on Monday and was able to go to her luncheon on Tuesday. It was a damn good thing, too, or who knows what else she might have said!

◆   ◆   ◆

Successful "dating" has not been a strong suit in our family. This next story is a compilation of several conversations I had with my grandmother, on the phone, or face to face, over a one-month period. My grandmother moved into a retirement community in 2002. As beautiful, charming, musical, and lively as she is, it's small wonder that she has had several potential suitors, none of whom seem to thrill her much. She was telling me about her woes with a gentleman in her retirement community who was "after her."

"You know, Karen, there's a man who's interested in me here," said my grandmother.

"Really. Tell me about him," I said, encouraging her to continue.

"I don't know that much about him. He doesn't talk right; he's not a good communicator. He won't leave me alone. I really don't want to have anything to do with him. He brought me cookies when he came back from Chicago for Thanksgiving. What should I do?" she explained.

"Thank him?" I offered.

"Well, of course I thanked him. He was in the dining room eating with his family last night, and I stopped by at his table to thank him. He introduced me to his whole family. They seem like nice people. But I want him to leave me alone. I am not interested in him or anyone else," she continued.

"OK, let me get this straight. You don't want to have anything to do with him, but you met his whole family? Don't you think you might be sending mixed messages?" I asked.

"You know what else he did? He took me out to dinner," she continued, totally ignoring my question.

I wanted to press her some more. I was curious about her rationale. "Wait a minute. You don't want to have anything to do with him, but you went out to dinner with him?" I asked.

"Well, I have to be polite, don't I? He asked me, so I went," she said.

"Did you have a nice time?" I asked.

"No. He's boring. He doesn't talk right. I can hardly understand him. He's a nothing. I have no feelings for him," she replied. "You know what else he did?" she went on. "He went out to breakfast one morning, came back, knocked on my door, and left. When I opened the door, there was a container waiting for me. It had a pancake in it that he had saved for me from breakfast."

I was really confused. Now it sounded as though she liked him and his flirtations, if you could call them that. "What did you do with the pancake?" I asked.

"I ate it," she answered smugly. "And you know what else he did?"

I wasn't sure I wanted to know. But, by now, curiosity had the best of me. "What did he do?" I inquired, playing along.

So, she told me, "He knocked on my door early one morning, and when I answered the door, he was just standing there looking at me."

Now the guy was irritating *me*. Was he an eighty-year-old stalker, and was he going to harm my grandmother? "What did he want?" I asked.

"He wanted a kiss!" she said with some exasperation.

Now my interest in the outcome of this story had resumed. I was sure Honey Anne was going to finally put the guy in his place. "What did you do?" I asked.

"I kissed him!" she answered.

I was bewildered. She wanted nothing to do with him, but she *kissed* him? "Why did you do that?" I asked, displaying more patience than I knew I had.

"Because he was standing there all puckered up! What could I do?" she explained.

I was getting tired of this. I thought she didn't like him. So I said, "You could have told him 'no' and closed the door on him."

"Well, it's done now. Anyway, I want him to leave me alone. He's a nothing," she went on.

"Now wait a minute. He can't be a nothing," I said, starting to defend a man that I hadn't even met, and a minute earlier I'd thought was a stalker.

"Why do you say he can't be a nothing?" she asked.

"Because, he obviously has good taste in women. He likes *you*," I replied.

My grandmother laughed like a schoolgirl, and I was finally on to her game. She liked the chase, and that was OK with me. But then she continued. "You understand. I don't have any feelings for him. I only had feelings for my husband. He was a wonderful man. I don't have feelings for other men. You understand that, don't you, honey?"

"Yes. I do understand that. Honey Joe was a wonderful man," I told her.

A few weeks after these conversations, my Aunt Joanie phoned me. "Karen, I have to tell you a story. I think you'll like it. I took your grandmother to the pain clinic yesterday. Did you know she has a man after her at the retirement community?"

"Oh, yes," I answered. "She's told me all about that situation."

"Well, you know she's not thrilled with him, right?" she asked.

"Umm hmm," I replied, "Yes, I know."

"Well, your grandmother was sitting in a long corridor waiting to be seen by a doctor. There were lots of other people in the corridor waiting to see doctors. Your grandmother was telling your uncle and me all about the man and how he won't leave her alone. Then she went into her 'I don't have any feelings for him. I only have feelings for my husband' routine. You know what I'm talking about?"

"Sure do. Heck, I was mouthing the words as you were saying them," I answered.

My aunt continued her story. "Then your grandmother, who doesn't speak very softly, mind you, tells your uncle and me, 'I'm going to become a *lesbian*!'"

I could hardly catch my breath I was laughing so hard. "What did you do when she said that?" I asked between guffaws.

"I laughed hard. Really hard," Aunt Joanie replied.

"Well what did all the people in the corridor do?" I wondered.

"It got really quiet in the hallway, and everyone, I mean EVERYONE looked our way," she answered.

"And what did Honey Anne do?" I asked.

"Oh, she kept right on talking. She never missed a beat," said my aunt.

Well, I know my grandmother and that guy have not become an item, and, as far as I know, I don't think my grandmother has become a lesbian. What I do know is that there are probably more 'grandmother stories' like this to come.

◆   ◆   ◆

I was tempted just to poke fun at my mother and grandmother in this book and leave it at that. I do believe that doing so would be totally unfair. Honestly, there are a lot of stories that I could tell about myself that would prove, even without DNA testing, that I am Anne's granddaughter and Micki's daughter. For your reading pleasure, the following are a select group of stories, detailing my funny contributions to family history. These stories might not be exactly related to the types of capers told in my mother and grandmother's sections of *I Never Meant to be Funny*, but I hope you still find them amusing.

Daughter (Karen) Stories

I'm sure evidence of my hereditary fate started at birth, but I just can't remember that far back. As a matter of fact, the first several years are kind of a blur. The first 'daughter story' I can recall was my initial attempt at sewing, outside of school and home economics class, that is.

I was thirteen and, as was common in our community, I was being invited to all sorts of Bar and Bat Mitzvah parties. Some were fancy and some were casual. I remember that my increase in social activities required buying a lot of new clothes (and taking dance lessons).

An upcoming Bar Mitzvah was going to be celebrated with a hayride party. My mother and I went out and bought new jeans and some tops to go with them. The jeans were too long, however, and since I'd just taken sewing in home economics, my mom suggested I shorten them myself.

My mom helped by pinning the pants, and then I got to the tasks of cutting and hemming. I worked diligently on the rust-colored jeans. I cut off the excess fabric and then hemmed the pants. When I tried them on, I thought I'd done a pretty good job. Filled with joy over my newly acquired skill, I started on the second leg of the jeans. Soon I was finished shortening my first pair of pants.

Proud of what I'd accomplished, I went into my room to try on the finished product. I couldn't wait to see my handiwork. I put the jeans on and soon realized I had not done such a very good job after all. Had I left some pins in the pants? Yeah, I'm sure I did. Was the hem crooked? Oh, yeah, probably. Were the legs uneven? Hell, yes! I'd cut and hemmed the same leg twice.

That one event 'shortened' my sewing career, too. My mom, after laughing at me (alone; I wouldn't be able to laugh at myself for many years yet), had to repair the rust-colored jeans and then shorten a second pair of new jeans, too. My mother has done most of my sewing jobs for me since.

◆   ◆   ◆

This next story is the first one that I can remember that deals with one of my passions—anything sports-related. I have always loved sports: participating in them and playing the role of spectator, too.

When I was younger, my Aunt Joanie and Uncle Paul owned a boat. I went out with them to the lake to swim, sun-bathe and have fun with the family. Everyone kept coaxing me to try water skiing, and I kept telling them, "No." I've tried it before, but I just can't seem to stay up on the skis. All I do is fall right back in the water. That's not too much fun. Thanks anyway."

After a few hours of prodding from my uncle, aunt, their friends, and my aunt's brother, I was ultimately persuaded to give it a try. My aunt's brother, Jay, and I were in the water, where he was giving me simple, easy-to-understand instructions. My uncle was seated in the boat, ready to go. Onlookers were providing me with such positive reinforcement, I actually began to believe I could do it. After a short lesson with Jay, and with a pounding heart, I heard myself say, "I'm ready!"

"Hit it!" yelled Jay to my uncle.

The boat took off and I felt myself pulled forward. I remember Jay telling me to 'just stand up,' so I did. It took some upper body strength to pull my butt out of the water, but, lo and behold, I was water skiing! I couldn't believe it! It was exhilarating! After countless attempts over many years, I had done it. And, it was only my first try of the day! I was having a really good time, but I thought I had better not press my luck. After we circled the lake once, I motioned to go back in.

I arrived back on shore to loud applause and shouts of approval. I felt like I had just won a big competition. I guess I had—me against my own fear.

I took a rest, and when asked later if I wanted to try it again, I said, "Sure." After all, with one full ride under my belt, I was a pro, right?

This time, it took a few attempts to get out of the water and up on the skis. We started to circle the lake, when about twenty seconds into the ride, the ski rope fell out of my hands. Natural athlete that I was, I caught the rope, of all places, between my legs. So, not only was I now a water-skier; I was a trick-skier, too!

"Oh, my God!" I said out loud. "What the hell am I doing? What the fuck do I do now?" (I told you I have a potty mouth when the situation seems right.)

'Should I continue around the lake and finish my ride?' I pondered. Should I stop right now and let the ride be over, or attempt a more difficult trick like a 'three-sixty?' All these thoughts were flashing through my brain. Never once, however, did I give serious thought to actually picking up the rope with my hands again. I thought if I did, I would wipe out big-time and that would be the end of the ride for sure.

After much debate inside my head, I thought it best to end this ride by widening my stance (actually, just moving my thighs out more laterally from my body). I figured the rope would fall harmlessly into the water and I would sink.

I put my plan into action and quickly found the faults in my thinking. My lack of flexibility did not allow me to widen my stance as much as I had anticipated, so the rope didn't just fall harmlessly into the water. It whipped me from crotch to knee on both legs before it finally plunged into the lake. And, I didn't sink, either. To add insult to injury, I toppled head first into the water.

"Are you OK?" asked my uncle as he circled the boat to get me.

"Yes," I answered with some embarrassment.

"Want to get up again?" he asked.

"Nope. I'm pretty sure I'm done for the day," I answered.

With a bruised ego and thighs to match, I climbed back into the boat. When I got back to shore, I saw only some tiny scratches on my thighs, and I really didn't feel any pain. Not only would I live, but figured that I'd be pretty darn fine, too.

This turned out to be another example of faulty thinking. Later that night while out to dinner with friends, I got up to use the bathroom. My thighs were suddenly very sore. That was strange, because they really hadn't bothered me all day. Walking was suddenly painful. How in the world was I going to squat and pee? Well, I managed, but it was tender, very tender. And, I noticed that those tiny scratches had turned into welts.

Over the next three weeks, those welts, from crotch to knee on both legs, blossomed into bruises of varying colors. My mother was embarrassed for me to sit at our condo's pool. She was sure people would think I'd been raped. "Don't worry, Ma. I'll correct them. I'll just tell them I've been *roped*," I said.

◆   ◆   ◆

The first time I remember, discovering to my horror, that I'd said something that sounded exactly like something my mother would say, was a few years ago. My friend Deb and I were going golfing with our friends Lynda and Steve. Deb and I drove to their house, then decided to go separately to the course, since Steve was anxious about getting there for our tee-off time.

Steve and Lynda raced off, speeding down the side streets and along main roads. Deb and I were going the normal speed limit, and, amazingly, we pulled up alongside of our friends' car, stopped at a red light about two miles from their house.

I turned to Deb and said, "Look at that! They're no farther ahead of us than we are."

She immediately started laughing, and I instantly put my hand over my mouth. "That was my mother that just came out of me, wasn't it?" I asked worriedly.

"Oh, yeah," Deb replied. "It sure was."

Funny, when I told my mom that story a day later, she saw neither the humor nor any need for concern. She said, "That sounds like something I would say."

"My point exactly, Ma. My point exactly!" I replied.

◆   ◆   ◆

I have a confession for you. I am quite mechanically challenged. On the few occasions when I am able to pull off something that even remotely resembles a mechanical, fix-it type achievement, I am as pleased as punch. When I don't fix something, it just adds to the list of failed attempts that grows every day. I share this particular ineptitude with my grandmother and mother, but *my* mechanical challenges have produced some funny 'daughter stories.' Here is one story where I combined two of my weaknesses and turned something simple into something needlessly more complex.

On the dresser in my bedroom, I had a television set, with a remote control. One day, all of a sudden, the remote just stopped working. The set itself was fine; I could manually turn it on and off, change channels, and work the volume. The set was fairly new, too, so I was bemused.

I reached in to those corners of my brain dedicated to mechanical aptitude, and pulled out the thought, "the remote must need new batteries." Yeah, that's an easy fix, I thought. I opened the remote to see what kind of batteries were needed, and I changed them. Placing myself in my Remote Control Activation Posture (one stands facing the set at a distance of about five feet, arms extended, aiming the remote at the set), I hit the ON button. Nothing! The thing still wasn't working. I was still befuddled.

"The replacement batteries must be old and dead," was the next tidbit I'd grabbed from my mechanical aptitude brain center. So, I went out and bought new batteries at the store. When I came home, I placed them in the remote, once more took my Remote Control Activation Posture and pressed the ON button. Again: nothing.

"Remember, you suck at this stuff." I questioned myself, "Are you sure you put the batteries in right?" Checking the batteries and the diagram within the remote, I discovered, yes, they were in there correctly.

I had reached my limit; I knew not what else to do. But wait! Oh, yes I did! I called on my friend Deb. She was mechanical, and she'd know what to do.

Deb took a look at the TV and the remote. She tried the remote and, again, nothing. I was relieved to see that it didn't work for her, either. She looked behind, underneath, on top of, and in front of the set.

"How long has the remote not been working, Karen?" Deb asked.

"Oh, about three weeks now," I answered.

"You've been doing some spring cleaning?" she inquired.

"Yeah, I changed my closets and drawers from winter to summer stuff. Why?" I replied. What did spring cleaning have to do with fixing my TV? (Another weakness: I'm not a very good cleaner, either.)

Deb then asked, "How long has the pile of shorts you have on the dresser been there?"

"About three weeks, I'd say," was my response. All of a sudden, I was starting to see a connection in her questioning.

In her kind and gentle way, Deb suggested, "Let's see what happens if we move these shorts away from in front of the TV, OK?" Deb put the shorts on my bed, hit the remote's ON button and, lo and behold, it worked.

That was when I first considered having friends handle my mechanical problems and housecleaning.

◆   ◆   ◆

Speaking of friends, my mother forms lasting friendships. Over the years, she has maintained friendships with people she knew in elementary school. I have many long-term alliances that are still going strong, too.

Do you remember the saying, 'what goes around comes around'? Well, for some of my friends and me, this next story, which spans a twenty-year period, proves the old saying well.

Back in the late 80s, I started teasing people when they had birthdays that ended in a zero. It all started when my friends Colleen and Dave both turned thirty. I thought it would be really funny if I went to a drug store and bought a whole bunch of personal care products for "old" people. I wanted to create a Survival Kit for turning thirty. I had a blast picking out digestive aids, corn and bunion protectors, hair coloring, and more. With every item I threw into my shopping cart, I chuckled. I formulated the words I'd write on little notes explaining to Colleen and Dave why I had specially selected each item for them. I do amuse myself so!

After wrapping all the gifts and writing funny notes for each one, I felt that there was still something missing. There had to be a key gift, one so clever it would make people laugh really hard. I pondered over this and finally decided on the perfect "I've Turned Thirty Survival Kit" enhancement. I'd get them each some gift certificates to a restaurant chain known for being attractive to senior citizens. The note attached to the gift certificates would read, 'so that you can be with your contemporaries.' I was really proud of myself for my creativity; the Survival Kit was complete.

A few weeks later, at a birthday bash, I presented the gift to Colleen and Dave. As always, they were gracious and enjoyed all of the gifts. They laughed a lot that night. As they thanked me, I saw a look of love in their eyes. They must have loved all the attention I'd just given them.

I always thought I was a planner, able to focus on the long-term as opposed to just what was happening tomorrow. Well, this time I sure wasn't too bright; I totally miscalculated. I never thought that my fun would come back to haunt me. I figured that Colleen and Dave would realize they couldn't top me, so why bother doing anything for *my* big birthdays? I was resting easy, but it was obvious to everyone else. Everyone at that party thought, 'What was she thinking? Karen's gonna get it right back when *she* turns thirty!' They couldn't have been more right. Looking back on it, that look of love in Colleen and Dave's eyes was probably a look of 'we'll get you, you little prankster.'

Another miscalculation on my part was introducing my friends Colleen and Dave to my friend Lynda. Once united, they became a deadly threesome. A year later, they threw me a surprise thirtieth birthday party which was, as far as I knew, merely a year-end softball party. I was very surprised. My family, non-softball playing friends, and my team were all there. They all wore buttons that read 'You're An Old Fart, Now' and other torturous statements. Lynda bought me a sweatshirt that said "I'm not 30; I'm 18 with 12 years of experience." There was a birthday cake with some awful saying about my old age. People bought me more personal care products for the aged than I knew existed. Lynda, Colleen and Dave, completely embarrassed me and definitely got even with me for what I started.

Ah, but the fun didn't stop there. Two days after the party, I went to work, where Lynda had made sure that my co-workers ripped on me the entire day. They had decorated my office in 'over-the-hill'-type decorations. There were copies of my baby pictures everywhere, compliments of my mother, (see, she gets *me* once in a while, too). When I got home from work that night, there was a ten-foot, wooden stork chained to the mailbox on my front lawn. Around its beak was a pink, wooden, baby blanket that read, "Karen Shulman: 30 years ago today." That damn stork was in my yard for over a month. Lynda kept telling me (lying to me was more like it) that the wooden stork company was coming any day to pick it up. Would it *never* end?

Did this create a truce between us? It did between Colleen, Dave, and I. But that left Lynda fair game, since she was solely responsible for the office pranks and the stork. She couldn't be too bright. Her fortieth birthday was only eight years away. That was a tremendous amount of time in which a planner might plan.

So here's the rest of the story: Time flies. A few months before Lynda's fortieth, I was at work and stopped in my coworker Marian's office to see how she was doing. Marian was a sweet woman who was usually very quiet and reserved, and she was always a polished professional. That day, Marian told me she had finally ordered a new clock. Her desk sat right outside my office, and faced a wall on which hung a battered, beat up old clock. Its face was creased, and it had been knocked on the floor so many times its crystal had long ago broken and been thrown away. It did, however, keep perfect time. "I've just become so sick of looking at that old thing, I had to order a new one," explained Marian.

"Good for you, Marian. What are you going to do with the beat up clock?" I asked.

Marian responded with, "I was going to throw it away, but if you have another idea, I'm open for suggestions. What are you thinking?"

"Well, we could send it to Lynda. She's going to be forty in a few months," I answered. My friend Lynda worked a few floors above us.

Marian got a huge gleam in her eye. "You want to? I think that's a great idea."

As I thought about it, I thought perhaps I should behave. Maybe I should just let sleeping dogs lie and let bygones be bygones. "No, I'd better not do it. It's a little early to start on Lynda, and if I do, I'll never hear the end of it. I'll get in big trouble with her. No, forget it, Marian. It's a bad idea. Forget I ever said anything, OK?"

I retreated back into my office and went back to work. About twenty minutes later, Marian came in and told me, "I think we have to send Lynda that clock. I found a box, some cellophane in which to wrap it, and a ribbon and bow to go around the box. Surely it's a sign. We have to send it to her!"

Marian was so excited about the idea, that I just hated to let her down. Besides, why not start the revenge on Lynda a few months early? She'd be hit totally off guard. I started to warm-up to the idea. "OK, Marian. Let's send it. But we have to put a note in with it," I said.

"What do you think the note should say?" Marian asked.

As we both thought about it, we moved to Marian's typewriter. We put our heads together and came up with, "This clock is 40-years-old. What will *you* look like when *you're* 40?" 'Perfect,' we both agreed; it was absolutely perfect. Much to Lynda's credit (because she'll be mad if I don't mention it) when she received it, she hung the clock and the note in her office for all to see. She thought it was funny, but she wasn't sure I was responsible, at least for a few days. And, she never believed me when I told her that Marian was in on it, too.

But the birthday game was on again. I kicked into high gear, thinking of ways to get Lynda on her fortieth. I learned that Lynda was going to be out of town for her birthday. She was combining work and personal time in a trip to California and would be gone two weeks. That just made things a whole lot easier for me: to have her out of town while I planned and plotted.

Much to my surprise, I did not have to work alone. I found so many others willing to be helpers. Lynda's grandmother gladly gave me baby pictures to hang all over the office. (OK, it's not original, but I liked it.) Her brother bowed out of picking her up from the airport when I told him I'd go get her. Her friends agreed to work with me on a project for greeting her at the airport upon her return to Toledo. Her friend Debbie even agreed to bake a cake for the surprise party. Her co-workers got busy decorating her office. More people than even I was aware of, were doing things to tease Lynda on her fortieth birthday. It had become an all-out team effort.

The night that Lynda returned to Toledo, several of her friends and I greeted her at the airport gate dressed up as old people. One friend wore an old man mask and looked like a 100-year-old. Another friend, Mary Jo, dressed up like Ruth Buzzy on Laugh-In—in a brown sweater and skirt, white blouse, thick hose, grandma shoes, and a hair net gathered in the center of her forehead. Mary Jo even put cabbages in her blouse to ensure that her breasts looked like they hung below her waistline. The effect was hysterical. I rented a walker, wore polyester pants and a sleeveless top that revealed bra straps hanging down my upper arms, and wore an old woman mask to cover-up my identity. We held signs that said: "40 Can Be Lonely; That's Why We're Here!" "LYNDA! NOTICE THE BIG PRINT? YOU ARE 40. IT SUCKS, DOESN'T IT?" and other such rudeness. It's a good thing this happened before 9/11/01, or we would never have made it past security; we'd have been asked to leave the airport and probably to never return.

As people came into the gate area from Lynda's flight, they chuckled and laughed at us. One couple stopped, looked at us, and asked, "Is it OK if we stick around and watch? This looks like it's going to be fun."

It *was* fun too. When Lynda finally came into the gate area, she looked up, saw us, turned a shade of red I never thought possible in a human, and started to turn around in an attempt to get back on the plane. "I don't know these people!" she yelled.

"Oh, yes, you do," we all sang out in unison, and Lynda gave in to our torture for the next several hours. We went back to my house for a surprise party, where more guests awaited. I don't remember many of the presents Lynda received, but I do remember Mary Jo getting her a can of 'Beard Buster.' That was pretty funny.

But the funniest stuff happened when Lynda went back to work. Her co-workers had removed the chair from behind her desk and replaced it with a wheelchair. There was literature from social security and mortuaries in her in-box. They had changed the week's cafeteria menu so that every dish had prunes in it (for example, cheeseburgers topped with prune whip). They had plastered her baby pictures in all the elevators and around her work floor. You could hardly get into her cubicle because of all the black streamers, balloons, and other decorations. They truly outdid themselves.

I got a call from Lynda the day she came back to work to find her office in disarray. "Did you send me the mortuary and social security information?" she asked.

"No, I've done a lot of things for your birthday, but I can't claim responsibility for those. Those are great ideas, though. Let me know who did it when you find out, OK?" I replied.

I found out who did it. Marian, that's who. She had so much fun with the clock, that she couldn't stop there. She had to keep going. She fessed up to me right away.

"Marian," I pleaded. "You're getting me in trouble. I got blamed for sending Lynda the mortuary and social security information. If you're planning on doing anything else, you have to stop! But I do want to tell you I'm so proud of you for doing what you did. Great work, my dear!"

Marian just stood there filled with pride. She was doubly excited to have tricked Lynda again and not been held responsible. Lynda has always thought I was a real heel to have blamed Marian for all these things. I'm not sure she ever believed it really was Marian behind those mailings.

I'm sure there were other things that we all did to make Lynda's fortieth very memorable; but honestly, I just can't recall all the details. I suspect that you're waiting for the 'what goes around, comes around' part. Don't worry; I haven't forgotten.

A few weeks after Lynda's birthday celebration, she called me. "Thank you for the AARP membership," she said to me in a snotty tone. (FYI: AARP is the organization formerly known as the American Association of Retired Persons.)

"AARP membership? What are you talking about, Lynda?" I replied, feigning ignorance.

"I got an AARP membership card in the mail. Thanks!" she said again in that snotty tone.

"What the heck are you blaming *me* for? I told you I was done, and I meant it." I said in my own defense. And I was done. I wasn't lying. I'd ordered that membership for her a month earlier. So what if I had changed her birth year on the application form to one twenty years earlier? I thought it was a hoot. But how did she know it was from me?

I found out when Lynda came in for the kill. Still in a snotty tone, she said, "My AARP card came with a note that said, 'compliments of Karen Shulman.'"

I was totally taken off-guard. "Why would it say that?" I inquired somewhat awkwardly.

In the snottiest tone she could muster, Lynda said, "Did you pay with a check?"

I was caught red-handed. "Why yes I did, Lynda. Shit! Yes, I did pay with a check."

I'd love to tell you that the rivalry stopped here, but, as I said at the beginning of this story, it is one that spanned approximately twenty years. Let's see, for my thirty-fifth, Lynda's husband wrote a newspaper-type article comparing my "longevity" to Cal Ripkin's and gave me more personal care products for one so aged. For my fortieth, Lynda and Steve gave me dead flowers, sent me about forty new *and used* birthday cards, and put my picture on the local Saturday morning news show. (Thank goodness they used a nice picture from their wedding.) And at fifty, I gave Lynda and Steve lifetime passes to a local fossil park, since they would be most comfortable with beings just like themselves. I also returned the personal care products Steve had given me for my thirty-fifth (yes, I saved them carefully for many years) with my own new commentary on each product.

I believe I can wait to see what's next, I really can. We have slowed down considerably (in many ways), but our minds are still sharp in terms of giving each other barbs. Remember, what goes around, comes around, and I'm the one with the next big birthday, so it looks like it's my turn next.

◆   ◆   ◆

Over the past few years, I have been working with an energy worker. If you don't know what an energy worker does, I'll try to explain briefly. Energy work, based upon the knowledge that the human body is energy, focuses on opening and clearing specific energy centers. In addition, energy work can include clearing and smoothing the layers of energy fields surrounding the body. Done primarily by laying hands above the body, it can also include some light touch. Additionally, there is talking between the energy worker and client that also helps to clear and smooth these energy centers and fields. I know this sounds a little strange, but I have discovered that it really works. Having gone through a few years of psychotherapy to move through issues, energy work has been comparatively faster and much more thorough in terms of getting results. It truly is amazing, and I hope you try it sometime.

Some energy workers have abilities beyond performing energy work. Some are psychics, clairvoyants, clairsentients, or clairaudients. My energy worker has bits of all those abilities, and, she also teaches me to be more in tune with seeing and feeling energy.

A part of energy work that often makes people quite suspicious is the energy workers' ability to see auras, or to see and speak to people who have 'crossed over' (died). And while I haven't mastered any aspect of energy work, especially the part about seeing auras or those who have crossed over, I have begun to feel energy more and believe that I have been able to communicate with those who have died.

All right, having said all that, and if I haven't wigged you out too much, let me remind you that there really is another 'daughter story' coming up. Just read on:

A while back, I went to Toledo's Valentine Theater to see a production. The Valentine is an old, downtown theater that was recently restored. This was my first visit there, and, before the production began, I was admiring the woodwork and painting, the tall ceilings, staircases, carpets and furnishings. The restoration of the theater was done beautifully.

I ventured downstairs to take in more of the building, and while there, I thought I would use the bathroom. It was brightly decorated in colorful tiles—red, white, yellow, and black. I 'did my thing' and then went to wash my hands. The sinks, faucets, and mirrors were all sparkling new. This was truly an impressive bathroom.

Looking into the mirror to my right, I saw a nicely dressed woman in a suit, beautifully made-up with her dark hair pulled back into a bun. Her reflection smiled back at me. I then looked out of the corner of my eye to my right, but I didn't see the woman. I figured she must have been standing farther back, perhaps in one of the stalls, in order to get a full view of herself. That's odd, I thought. Discretely, I turned slightly to my right to see if, in fact, she was standing in one of the stalls. She wasn't; she was nowhere to be found. Then I looked back in the mirror, and there she was again!

This was getting a little freaky, and I was getting a little puzzled. Next, I saw her in the mirror, moving away from the sinks and walking toward me. If I looked down now, at the ground, I'd be sure to see her shoes. But when I looked down, I saw no feet moving my way. Now I was totally perplexed. How could I see her in the mirror but then not see her physically? 'Hot damn,' I thought. 'All that energy work is rubbing off on me. I do believe I've *seen* my first "spirit." In fact, I was almost sure of it. What else could possibly explain what I'd just seen? I was pretty excited, and couldn't wait to go tell my friends upstairs what had just happened.

I finished washing my hands and then walked around the other side, to the other set of stalls, in order to exit the bathroom. I glanced over at the sinks and mirrors on that side and realized that I was still a novice at seeing spirits.

Above each sink was a mirror, but between each sink was a space that looked across to the sinks on the other side. The woman I had seen hadn't been a spirit from the 'other side' at all. She was just a woman who was washing her hands and looking into a mirror on the *other side of the bathroom*. I chuckled at myself as I thought, "I am my mother's daughter. My mother sees dancers who are, in reality, umbrellas. I see a spirit from beyond who is actually a living person!"

As I made my way to the steps to go back upstairs, I saw the woman whose "reflection" I'd seen in the bathroom. Walking up to her I said, "You *are* real, after all. You had me scared back there in the bathroom. I thought you were a figment of my imagination."

She smiled brightly, grabbed my arm and said, "I know what you mean. I didn't think *you* were real, either." We both shared a laugh, smile, and sigh of relief.

When I went back upstairs, the story I told to my friends was quite different than my first experience seeing a spirit. It was just another spirited 'daughter story.'

◆   ◆   ◆

While we're on the subject of bathrooms, the following is a classic example of the lesson my mother taught me: it's OK to laugh at yourself. Here is a very funny and embarrassing story that took a few years before I could tell it about myself:

I live in Ohio, but I grew up in Michigan. In the part of Michigan, where I grew up, port-a-potties were often designated as male or female. I never understood the difference, or why there was a need for separate port-a-potties. Going to the bathroom in a large hole seemed pretty straightforward, so to speak, regardless of sex. However, some things you just don't question. When I moved to Ohio, a port-a-potty was simply a port-a-potty. Men and women used the same ones, and I was satisfied with this new scenario.

I had occasion to use a port-a-potty in Ohio at the Jamie Farr LPGA Golf Tournament. One of the first spectators out for that day's round of golf, I was eager to watch the tournament. Hurriedly, I made my way to get a pairing sheet and a copy of the official event magazine. After watching a couple of pairings tee off on hole number one, I walked toward the back of the Highland Meadows Golf Course. While walking, I realized that perhaps the hole I'd just been watching had sent me a subliminal message: I had to go Number One.

Finding a unisex port-a-potty nearby, I went inside. It was very clean, and smelled fresh; I must have been the first one in there that day. I noticed that it had some added features, too, ones I had not been familiar with back in Michigan. It had a hand sanitizer dispenser, wet wipes, and even a purse shelf. I used the purse shelf to hold my magazine, finished going to the bathroom, cleaned my hands, picked up my magazine, and went back out on the course.

As Mother Nature would have it, a few hours later, I had to use a port-a-potty again. This time, I did not enter one that was so freshly clean. It still had the hand sanitizer dispenser, wet wipes, and purse shelf. Only this purse shelf was wet. And the wetness wasn't water. It was colored. Yellow, maybe?

"Oh, my God!" I yelled out loud. "That's not a purse shelf. It's a damned urinal! Disgusting!" I finished in a hurry, washed my hands, then ran to the nearest wastebasket. Trust me, I threw away my magazine and then went back to the port-a-potty to wash my hands again.

So much for Ohio port-a-potty amenities. I think I like Michigan's much better, after all.

◆   ◆   ◆

This very good 'daughter story' occurred when I was trying to play a practical joke on my mother. This one wasn't exactly my idea, but I certainly went along for the ride.

My first-cousin Mindy called to chat one day. Mindy has a very keen wit, and she always makes me laugh. We spent some time catching up on one another's lives and then she asked me if I'd like to help her start a rumor in the family. "A rumor?" I asked. "What kind of rumor?"

"Oh, I don't know. I'm thinking it has to be something outrageous that might get back to us after it made the rounds in the family," she answered.

"You have something in mind already, don't you?" I questioned.

"No, not really. Think of something, Kar," she suggested.

"I'm not that quick, Min. I'd need some time to think about it. You're the pro here. I'm only an amateur. Surely you have something in mind," I repeated.

"Well, OK, yes. You know how my mom is going through a divorce, and, you know how outrageous my mom can be?" she offered.

Mindy's mom, Maggie, had recently been remarried, and after about a year-and-a-half of 'marital un-bliss,' Maggie was divorcing her husband. Maggie can be very extreme sometimes; so "outrageous" was an understandable description. "Umm hmm," I said. "Go on."

"Well. What if we told someone in the family that now my mom has to have a tattoo of her soon-to-be ex removed from her body?" Mindy inquired.

"What's the tattoo of, and where is it?" I asked.

"What it is—well, let's leave that to everyone's imagination. And, let's say it's on her ass. What do you think, Kar?" replied Mindy.

"Well, I'd like to know who we're going to start the rumor with, so that I can tell you if I think it'll fly," I said. In my head I was hoping she'd say it'd be best to start with my mother.

As if reading my mind, Mindy suggested, "How about your mother?"

"I think I can sell it," I replied, "if I package it correctly. Let me run with it, and we'll see where it goes. I'll let you know when the seeds have been planted." I told her.

"Kar, I'm going to call my mom and let her in on it, too, OK? That way, if your mom should happen to call her and ask, Maggie will be prepared to play her part," contributed Mindy.

"OK. This is going to be funny. Talk to you soon. Love you, Min. Say hi to your hubby and the kids for me, OK?" I said.

"Love you too, Kar," Mindy replied, and hung up.

It took me a while to figure out just how to present this story to my mom. I was tempted to call her right away, but figured I'd laugh and spoil the joke. Over the next two weeks I spoke with her by telephone and still could not muster up the nerve to start the practical joke. Finally, about three weeks after Mindy's and my original conversation, I sent my mom an email that went something like this:

> Ma, I've been meaning to ask you. Do you know anything about Aunt Maggie and a tattoo of her ex? I hear Aunt Maggie has to have a tattoo, that's ex-husband-related, removed from her body now that they're going through a divorce. Have you heard anything about this? Let me know what you know. I know this sounds a bit strange, but this is what I've heard. And, you know Aunt Maggie…
>
> Love, Karen

About a day later, my mom sent me an email response. This is a summary of what she wrote:

> No, I haven't heard anything about your Aunt Maggie's tattoo. I'm not sure that she'd tell me about anything like that. She doesn't tell me much these days. You see, I told her not to marry that guy. And I told her not to sign a pre-nuptial agreement. And I suggested she not sell her house and move. But, your Aunt didn't listen to me. So, she probably wouldn't tell me about a tattoo. Do you know where it is and what it is? You probably know more than me. Write me back soon with more details. This is verrrrrrrrrrrrrrrrrrrrrrrrrrrry interestingggggggggggggggggg!
>
> Love, Mom

To say the least, when I read that email, I was overjoyed. The hook had been baited and Mindy and I were on our way. I couldn't wait to tell her! So I sat down at the computer, took my mom's response, edited it a bit, and forwarded it to Mindy. The subject of the email was *I Think We Got Her.* I expected to hear back from Mindy very soon. She leaves her computer on all the time, so I knew she'd see my email. I kept checking my new emails all day, but there was nothing from Mindy. She was probably busy with the kids. I'd have to wait.

The following day, my mother called me. "So, the thing with Aunt Maggie is a joke, huh?" my mom asked accusingly.

I was very puzzled. Trying to buy time I replied, "What?" (I know. Good response, eh? Yeah, and it didn't buy me any time, either.)

"The thing with Aunt Maggie and the tattoo. It's a falsehood, isn't it?" she continued to hammer me.

"A falsehood?" I laughed. I hadn't heard *that* word used in a spoken sentence, probably ever. I was growing more confused. Had Mindy double-crossed me? Was the practical joke actually on me? If so, I would really get her back. But that just couldn't be. We were partners in this joke. Mindy wouldn't turn on me. So what the hell was going on? This was supposed to be funny, but I was being backed into a tight little corner, and it wasn't funny any more. "What are you talking about, Ma?" I asked, trying to stall for time once more.

"The email you sent," as she came in for the kill.

Uh-oh. Now I had a sinking feeling. I was almost sure Mindy was a traitor. "Which email would that be, Ma?" I asked.

"The one titled *I Think We Got Her?*" she said, booking me on an all expenses paid guilt trip.

"You got *that* email? How did you get that email, Ma?" I asked.

"You sent it to me. You sent it to me and Mindy!"

All sorts of thoughts started racing through my head. Shit! How could I have sent that email to *her*? That just wasn't possible. Mindy must have sent it to her. No, Mindy wouldn't do that. Then I must have sent it to her. How in the hell did I send that email to her? Crap! I had ruined the practical joke. The truth was staring me in the face (well, in the ear, since we were on the phone). "*I* sent that email to you?" I asked awkwardly.

"Yes, you did. I wasn't supposed to get it, was I? Is this your idea of a joke, or was this all Mindy's idea, and you just played along?" my mother asked, her tone brightening hopefully.

Here was the perfect opportunity to lie. I could pin this all on Mindy and just walk away clean. But I couldn't do it; I had to fess up. "Ma," I explained. "Mindy and I both did this. It was 50-50. I'm just as responsible for this as she is."

"What if I'd asked your Aunt Maggie about this? What would've happened then?" my mom asked.

"Umm. Well, Aunt Maggie was in on it, too. Mindy clued her in, and she was prepared to tell you I-don't-know-what. But she'd have played along," I answered.

"What if I would have told your grandmother?" my mother asked in all sincerity.

I didn't see that as a real big deal, so I offered, "You'd have untold her."

My mom didn't like my tone. "This was supposed to be *funny*? This was a practical joke? But you *never* play practical jokes on me!"

"You've got to be kidding, Ma!" I quipped back. "I *always* play practical jokes on you. What are you talking about?"

The debate was on. "What if I would have pretended never to have seen that email, *I Think We Got Her*? I could have played this to the very end with you and Mindy thinking you had me, and then I could have turned it on you. What about that?" she snipped back.

She had a point. In fact, she had a very good point. Any practical joker worth their salt could see that there was beauty in her envisioned plan. But I had to have the last word. I had to save face. I needed to redeem myself, but I also needed to give her some credit. So I said, "Ma, That would've been good, and you probably could have pulled it off. Maybe next time you'll be wise enough to do that."

"There *will* be a next time, Karen. And I promise, you won't be expecting it, and it will be good. Just beware. You'd better watch it. I will get you back," she threatened.

My mom's threatening words are still hovering in the air. She hasn't struck yet, but I'm watchful. One of these days, my mom will get me back.

We hung up soon thereafter. I raced to my computer and logged on to the Internet, to find out what I did. How could I have sent her that email? I quickly got into my sent mail folder and found the *I Think We Got Her* email. I opened it and saw that I had never even sent it to Mindy; I'd *only* sent it to my mother. It was one of those 'I should have hit "Forward" instead of "Reply"' mistakes. A very costly mistake, and now I had to break the news to Mindy.

I re-forwarded the *"I Think We Got Her"* email to Mindy with a new title *"I Am My Mother's Daughter."* It had an introductory statement that went something like this: *I'm afraid I have bad news! The tattoo joke is off. I accidentally sent my mother this email instead of you. She just phoned me and called me out on the carpet. She knows the whole story now. What can I say? The only logical explanation is that I am my mother's daughter. I am really sorry. Love, Kar.*

Later that night, Mindy called me. "Kar, I got your email a few hours ago. It's taken me this long to stop laughing so that I could dial the phone and talk to you. I agree. You *are* your mother's daughter, and you *are* an idiot!"

◆   ◆   ◆

I'm an avid sports fan and consider myself a pretty decent athlete, too. I have been able to reach some level of proficiency in softball, basketball, volleyball, tennis, football, and bowling (not to mention water skiing). Golf, however, has been one sport that can be classified as 'not my game.' Sure, I know if I played it more, I could become a much better player. You know what I say to that? I need to play it better to want to play it more. Sounds like a 'catch 22' to me. Nonetheless, I do get out and golf a few times each summer, but I have to admit, I enjoy being outdoors and socializing with friends and family a lot more than the golf itself.

A few summers ago, my friends Lynda and Steve asked me to join them for a round of nine holes. I searched for an excuse but I had absolutely nothing else to do, so I said yes. It was a chilly day, so we decided to hit some range balls before starting our round. Bedford Hills Golf Course has a nice range where the practice tee boxes have dividers made of wood and screen fabric. When Lynda, Steve and I got there, the range was fairly empty, so I took a tee box toward the left, Lynda was two boxes from me on my right, and Steve was two boxes beyond Lynda.

I was about two-thirds of the way through my bucket of range balls when a man arrived and soon occupied the stall directly to my left. I get a bit anxious about my golf anyway, so it didn't help having somebody right next to me. There were several other tee boxes available. Why did this guy have to come right next to me to hit golf balls?

Trying to bury my anxiety and agitation, I started hitting again. So did the guy next to me. I never looked at him, but, he sounded like he was big, and though he was hitting the ball really hard, it didn't sound like he was hitting too well. That made me relax a bit. He hit; the ball went off with a thudding sound. I hit; the ball never quite made it into full flight. Occasionally, one of us would hit the wooden partition between the boxes if we hit a really awful shot. In my mind, I thought the stranger was hitting much worse than I. That honestly made me feel better about my lack of 'game.'

When I bent over to get another ball, a stray golf ball suddenly came whipping from behind me, nearly nailing me in the foot. Then it rolled into the bucket. Here were my immediate thoughts:

> Wow! I've hit some pretty piss-poor shots in my day, but nothing like what the guy next to me just hit. That shot just sucked. How the hell did he hit that ball under the wooden divider and screen? He must have put some real power into that practice swing to get it past all those barriers. Oh my God! And then he almost hit me in the foot. He could've broken my foot with that shitty shot! And, I can't believe this: the ball he hit was a white ball, and the range balls are yellow. This guy must not know a friggin' thing about golf. He's hitting his own balls on the driving range. OK, do I say something to him or not? Oh my gosh! What would I even say? 'Here's your ball back, sir. Maybe it's best you not play, sir. You obviously don't know shit about golf.' No, it's best if I just stay quiet. If he wants his ball back, he'll ask.

So, I started hitting a few more shots. With about four practice balls remaining, I started thinking about the guy next to me again. 'I bet he's playing with some really fancy golf balls, too. Probably Pinnacles.' Curiosity got the best of me. I just had to peek at what kind of golf balls were being used by this really dreadful golfer next to me. I bent down and picked up his white ball. 'Some big burly guy, who's an awful golfer, uses Breast Cancer Awareness golf balls? I use Breast Cancer Awareness golf balls, too,' I thought.

That's when I realized that that golf ball that came whipping from the tee box next to me wasn't from the tee box next to me at all. It was a Breast Cancer Awareness golf ball that had shot out of my own sweater pocket.

That was one time I was really glad I kept my thoughts to myself.

As a side note: I laughed at myself, and I couldn't wait to tell Lynda and Steve what I had done. When I started to tell them, I was laughing so hard I was almost crying. Lynda said, "Oh, this must be good. Did you just do something stupid? Because that's what your expression is saying." I told them the story, and I've told it to lots of others since then.

You see I *am* like my mother. When I do a 'daughter story,' I just can't keep it to myself.

Conclusion

When we are children, we laugh at many things, and life is an amusing game. When we become adults, often times, for many of us, we lose some of our innocence and zest for life. We forget about the little things that bring us joy and laughter, things that could lighten our lives.

If there is anything my mother understands about living life as an adult, it is the importance of reclaiming childhood simplicity. In Micki's world there is always laughter. Whether battling illness, being a mother, or just managing everyday life, she tries to keep things playful. Maybe she has an advantage, having been a kindergarten teacher, but I don't think that's the secret, because for my mother, laughter has always been a key component in her life.

My wish for you, reader, is that you find the laughter in *your* everyday life. I don't think you'll have to look that hard; it's all around you.

Just the beginning, I'm sure. Not

The End

Do You Have A Funny 'Mother Story' Of Your Own To Share?

I know I'm not the only one with a funny mother. Your mother is probably very funny in her own right. Please share some stories with me.

If you would like to contribute a story for a future volume of *I Never Meant to be Funny* about your mom (or somebody else's, for that matter), please send it to:

motherstories@aol.com

Don't forget to include your name, address, phone number, and email address with your submission. We'd like to be able to contact you.

If we use your story in a future version of *I Never Meant to be Funny*, you will be credited for your creation. Thank you so much for wanting to record your story for posterity and make others laugh.

0-595-30596-2

Made in the USA
Lexington, KY
03 December 2012